NATIVE AMERICAN HISTORY *of* WASHINGTON, DC

Armand Lione, PhD

The History Press

Published by The History Press
Charleston, SC
www.historypress.com

First published 2023

Manufactured in the United States

ISBN 9781467154215

Library of Congress Control Number: 2023937173

Notice: The information in this book is true and complete to the best of our knowledge. It is offered without guarantee on the part of the author or The History Press. The author and The History Press disclaim all liability in connection with the use of this book.

This book is dedicated to the people in and around Washington, DC, who hope to learn more about the other people who lived here for centuries before colonists arrived and the Metro was built.

Contents

Acknowledgements

Native Land Acknowledgement

This book was written while the author lived in Washington, DC, on the original land of the Anacostan People of the Piscataway Tribe.

Personal Acknowledgements

This book would not have been written without the encouragement, cooperation and help from a great many people. My first presentation on DC's Native American history was attended by only two guests, John Capozzi, a DC political activist whom I've known for many years through Ultimate frisbee games, and Nick Griffin, also originally a frisbee friend. During the last few years, Nick and his partner, Rochelle Davis, have become my go-to advisors on many issues that are discussed in this book.

It was Ruth Trocolli, the archaeologist of the District of Columbia, who suggested I create a group with a social media presence to expand my efforts. Ruth has a deep awareness of the Native history of the city, and her encouragement has been very important to me. Her helpful suggestions led to the formation of the DC Native History Project (DCNHP).

Key people who contributed time to the Facebook site for the DCNHP included Ben Aaronson, whose graphic talents were invaluable, and Bob Engelman, who had many good organizational and practical suggestions. Matthew Dull and James Salt have helped me investigate the history of the

Piney Branch quarry site and are active in promoting its public recognition. Donovan Kuehn, a friend and neighbor, has also patiently listened to tales about my work and made insightful suggestions for new directions to develop. His wife, Sara Willi, generously used her talents to shoot my author photo.

Chief Jesse James Swann, Matriarch Julie Tayac Yates and Dr. Peter Ufland also generously gave their time to write the kind forewords for this book.

Help from my longtime friend Leanne Mitchell, in Melbourne, Australia, was instrumental in getting permissions from Aboriginal leader Uncle Shane Charles and the Port Phillip EcoCentre to include the *Once As It Was Map of Melbourne* in this book.

Thanks to the Arts Club of Washington, whose president, Henry Sienkiewicz, and member Bob Craycraft provided me with a choice opportunity in 2021 to present and refine many of my collected stories in an important public forum.

With the use of their excellent skills in searching for old news reports that contained information on the Native history of Washington, amateur historians Mark Herlong and Hayden Wetzel generously provided me with the nineteenth-century news articles on the Native canoe found near the Navy Yard and fishing village remains on Buzzard Point. Longtime friend and geographer Jon Price contributed important insights about the canoe's deep underground location.

Miriam Doutriaux of the Smithsonian Anacostia Community Museum allowed me to inspect and photograph local Native American artifacts. Richard Tehaan and other members of the Friends of Fletcher's Cove (https://savethecove.org/) identified historic photos of an important local dig and provided me with usable images.

Others who kindly gave permissions to reprint their work in this book include James Krakker, Dan Dalrymple, Doug Dupin and Edward Haile.

Peter Tyler, an old friend who is a prolific short story writer, volunteered to do the first edits of the text. Kate Jenkins, my editor at The History Press, repeatedly surprised me with her extensive help creating usable images as well as her insightful commentary on the text. Abigail Fleming, also a History Press editor, provided the final supportive input that brought this book to print.

David Grosso, who set such an excellent example of how a DC city councilperson should publicly acknowledge Native American history, also generously gave of his time to contribute his perspective on how more can be done to celebrate the Native history of this city.

Content warning: A few images show burial sites that include human remains.

FOREWORDS

A world-class scholar, a tireless advocate for Native history and a compassionate individual with a heart for improving the lives of First People's communities today. These and many more are apt descriptions of Dr. Armand Lione.

I first met Armand when I reached out to the DC Native History Project in 2019. At that point, I and the Piscataway Conoy Tribe community had already been working tirelessly on many projects, including, but not limited to, petitioning for a restoration of our treaty rights that had been guaranteed by a 1666 treaty—Treaty of Peace and Amity—for four years. Inviting the Piscataway Indian Nation to join us, we had also been working to redress the policy of robbing tribal members of their identity by precluding the designation of Native American on DC birth certificates. I will always be grateful for Armand's embrace of our projects. It was he who facilitated critical first meetings that eventually led to a bill being passed that made both goals a reality in 2022.

Chief Jesse James Swann, Piscataway Conoy Tribe. *Photo by Rosanna Swann.*

I have had the pleasure of collaborating with Armand on several other projects. These include an acknowledgement by the DC Public Library that it stands on stolen Piscataway land and an ongoing commitment to shine a spotlight on Native stories that are not often visible. Together with his sterling scholarly work, Armand's long personal history of being a true ally to the area's First People's communities enrich *The Native American History of Washington, DC* and make it a book eminently worth reading.

Chief Jesse J. Swann Jr.
Chief of the Piscataway Conoy Tribe

I want to express my appreciation of Dr. Armand Lione for his knowledge and interest in the Indigenous people of the Washington, DC area, including my tribe, the Piscataway Indian Nation.

Matriarch Julie Tayac Yates, Piscataway Indian Nation. *Photo by author.*

Our work together over the past two and a half years has already made a remarkable impact by highlighting the history of the Native people who lived in the District, Maryland and Virginia over four hundred years ago, as we still do today. During that time, we've worked with the DC City Council on a fishing rights bill for Native Americans; a land acknowledgement for the newly rebuilt central DC public library; and meetings with representatives of DC Water and the Bolling Air Force Base to work on their acknowledgement of the Native history of land they now occupy.

I look forward to continuing my work with him on the history of the original inhabitants of our land, and I wish him great success with this book!

Matriarch Julie Tayac Yates
Piscataway Indian Nation

Twelve years ago, when I was first asked to teach a course on the history of the District of Columbia, I was confronted by a rather surprising challenge. Having taken a broad range of urban history courses during both my master's and doctoral programs, I assumed that there would be any number of readily available published monographs on the

District of Columbia, as well as a concise, up-to-date, college-level textbook that would effectively cover the breadth of the city's history. Contrary to my assumption, the few general histories of DC that I found were either intended for lower grade levels or antiquated. As a result, I spent the next several years scrambling to put together a patchwork array of published and online materials that would meet the needs of my courses at the University of the District of Columbia.

Over a decade later, I have come to realize that the challenge that I encountered stemmed from several underlying factors. One of the most important of these is the broadly accepted public perception that nothing really existed in the locale that is now the District of Columbia prior to the establishment of the city as the nation's capital. Or to put it another way, anything that occurred before the founding of the capital is and was viewed as largely unimportant.

The introduction to the second chapter of Chris Myers Asch and George Derek Musgrove's *Chocolate City: A History of Race and Democracy in the Nation's Capital* alludes to this very point. Noting that tour guides often erroneously tell visitors that the city was built on a swamp, *Chocolate City* correctly points out that the land that would become the District of Columbia was not only populated but also occupied by several tobacco plantations worked by enslaved laborers. Given the focus of their book, Asch and Musgrove no doubt meant to highlight the fact that, to this very day, the centrality of race and slavery in the city's history has been at best downplayed and at worst ignored altogether. In a larger sense, though, the vignette, which I refer to in my course as "the myth of a swamp," also suggests that the presence of plantations, farms, warehouses and enslaved people is that much easier to ignore because, as the story goes, there was nothing here before the arrival of the capital.

Chocolate City has done much to alleviate the challenge that I encountered when I first began teaching my class on the history of the District of Columbia. It not only provides an outstanding overview of the history of the city but also goes a long way to ensuring that our understanding of the District of Columbia, and perhaps the nation in general, is firmly fixed on the integral relationship between race and power. In doing so, it manages to fill in key aspects of the untold history of our nation's capital.

And yet, there is still far too much of DC's history that remains largely hidden. One particularly problematic lacuna within the history of the District of Columbia is that concerning the Indigenous people of the area. Arguably, no other aspect of the story of the land that would become the nation's capital and the people who lived there has been so ignored.

In the same way that the "myth of a swamp" obscures the long history of race and slavery that defined the area prior to the founding of the capital, so too does it help obliterate the existence of the Native peoples who lived, for thousands of years prior to the arrival of Europeans and enslaved Africans, on the land that would become the District of Columbia. The failure to recognize the Indigenous communities of the area or examine their history, however, goes far beyond a lack of academic research or published work. Rather, it includes an almost complete lack of public awareness of the fact that Indigenous communities dotted the landscape of today's DC and a dearth of public markers or memorials recognizing their existence.

Perhaps no one has done more to correct the shameful failure to recognize the history of the Indigenous communities of Washington, DC, than Dr. Armand Lione. I first met Dr. Lione by complete happenstance, as we both reside in the same part of Capitol Hill. Ever since, Dr. Lione has graciously visited my DC history class each semester to help educate my students in an area of local history that I was woefully unprepared to do myself. Dr. Lione has not only helped my students gain greater knowledge of the Indigenous peoples who lived in the area but also helped to further dispel the "myth of the swamp" by filling in a vital aspect of DC's forgotten or, perhaps more accurately, ignored history.

Of course, Dr. Lione's efforts to bring the history of DC's Native peoples to its proper place in the forefront of the city's story include far more than just visiting my classes. He has published articles, maintained the DC Native History Project webpage and utilized every available outlet to further educate the public about the Native communities that existed in the area. He has also advocated for greater public recognition of these peoples by the city and federal governments and fought for more prominent coverage of the city's Indigenous communities at the National Museum of the American Indian.

In writing this book, Dr. Lione furthers his efforts to ensure that the history of the Indigenous peoples of DC is no longer relegated to the "swamp." Offering both broad coverage and precise detail, Dr. Lione's book provides insight into the various Indigenous communities and sites that once occupied the land that is today Washington, DC. In addition, he tells the story of those communities, their encounters with European colonizers and the all too familiar tragic process that led to their abandonment of the area.

Perhaps just as importantly, Dr. Lione brings much-needed attention to the numerous excavations, over more than a century, of Native American

Peter Ufland. *Courtesy of Peter Ufland.*

sites and artifacts in DC. In doing so, he highlights the fact that despite this past work and the artifacts that it has produced, the Native past remains, by and large, unknown to even lifelong residents of the city. As Dr. Lione correctly points out, this lack of awareness is, in no small part, due to the lack of formal historical markers celebrating the city's original inhabitants.

Dr. Lione's *Native American History of Washington, DC* is a book that is long overdue. While Indigenous American history in general has received considerably greater attention over the past two decades, the growing depth and richness of this field has not included particular focus on the Native communities of DC. Through careful, detailed research, broad topical coverage and insightful analysis, this book helps correct the historical record on DC's Native past. One can only hope that the book, along with Dr. Lione's continuing advocacy, will further fill in the "myth of the swamp" and allow for a more accurate understanding of the history of our nation's capital.

Dr. Peter Ufland
Associate Professor of Liberal Studies
University of the District of Columbia Community College

PREFACE

In 1918, Margaret Brent Downing wrote an article for the *Washington History Journal* on the nineteen landowners who negotiated with George Washington to provide the land that became Washington, DC.[1] As an aside in her introduction, she noted:

> *Few cities of the larger and more cultured class have displayed a greater indifference towards the original owners of the land on which it has been built than the National Capital.*

Well, Maggie Downing, it's sad to say, but now, over one hundred years later, your comment still rings true!

The history of the Native Americans in Washington is not part of the fundamental story of this city. I'd lived in Washington for more than thirty years with a typical neglect of the First People who lived here, until 2016, when I first asked, "Who were the Indigenous people of the District of Columbia?"

Like the history of the Afro-American slaves that built much of the city, including the White House,[2] the stories of the Native people who lived on this land for several thousand years before English settlers arrived rarely get acknowledged in our daily lives.

Most of the time I've lived in Washington, I've worked as a reproductive toxicologist. I moved here in 1979 after getting a doctorate in pharmacology and toxicology at the University of Rochester. Very fortunately for me, the DC organization I worked for, the Reproductive Toxicology Center (Reprotox), was designed to be an *online* database of published information about the possible harmful effects of drugs and chemicals on pregnancy.[3]

During the 1990s, the internet grew and the Reprotox database was put entirely online for remote access by members from individual computers. These changes made it possible for me to update our agent summaries on drugs and chemicals remotely as new reports became available.

Working out of my house in the early 2000s, it didn't take me long to consider how I might try to work from other locations and live in warmer spots during the winter. In 2004, I went to Sydney, Australia, from January to March. At that time, for me to upload my work and send it back to Reprotox, I had to go to an internet café and do a special setup with the help of the café staff. The process was a little complicated, but it was doable! Because I wasn't sure I could work from Australia, I hadn't told my co-worker and the director of Reprotox, Dr. Tony Scialli, about my trip. I figured, if I couldn't work, I'd just take the time as an extended vacation. After emailing Tony my work for a week or so from Australia, he commented, "You're working odd hours!" I hadn't allowed for the twelve-hour difference in time zones and just sent off my work after I finished my half day of updating our summaries. Tony was happy for me to be in Australia that year, but that experience got Tony to check with me for several following winters, asking, "Where are you now?"

In the early 2000s, using the internet to transfer data quickly became very easy. I remember that for a few years, when I searched for places to overwinter in new cities, rental apartments would emphasize the availability of Wi-Fi, but internet access quickly became an assumed amenity.

Since it was rather easy to work from anywhere, I went away each winter after 2004 and started going back to Australia in 2008. My Australian friend Leanne Mitchell, who first got me started visiting there after she moved back in 2003, visited Washington in 2007 and told me she had moved to Melbourne and encouraged me to visit. I did that in 2008 and discovered a wonderful city! As it turned out, I went back to Melbourne every other year (2010, 2012, 2014, 2016, 2018) until 2020.

You don't have to live in Australia for long before you get exposed to a concern about their Indigenous people. On February 13, 2008, about one month into my first visit to Melbourne, the Australians did their first "National Apology" to their Indigenous People, presented to the Australian Parliament by Prime Minister Kevin Rudd.[4] It was a public holiday in 2008 and is now marked each year on February 13. This, by the way, is in addition to their annual event on May 26 of National Sorry Day, which has been held since 1998.[5]

In 2016, shortly after I got back from wintering in Melbourne, I was sitting in a playing field in southwest DC, waiting for a frisbee game to start, and I looked around and began asking, "Who were the Indigenous people who originally lived here in Washington?"

An additional focus for my original searches on the Native people of DC was the question of whether they were displaced in order to make way for the Capital City. It turned out, as I'll explain in detail later, they were displaced by pressure from local settlers more than one hundred years before the city was planned.

When I started researching the Native American history of Washington, I quickly realized that it isn't very hard to find information about the tribe that once lived here, the Anacostans. Online searches quickly led me to the Library of Congress (LOC). Fortunately, I live only a few blocks from the LOC. You can get access to a lot of their sources online, but going to the library offers access to a lot more.

A key figure who rapidly popped up in my LOC searches was one archaeologist from the 1880s, Samuel Vincent Proudfit. Before moving to Washington, DC, Proudfit had done archaeological research in Missouri on the Native Americans who built mounds along the Mississippi River, in and around St. Louis.[6] In the 1880s, Proudfit took a desk job at the Department of the Interior, here in Washington, which didn't primarily involve archaeology. In his spare time, however, Proudfit wandered around various parts of Washington searching for artifacts that indicated a history of Native life. As is explained in detail in chapter 2, Proudfit commented in his writings on how pleased he was by the many Native sites he could find around the city. Over more than a decade, Proudfit collected and recorded many of his finds and published reports on his work, which included maps showing Native village sites and quarries. This map, published in 1930 as part of congressional symposium on the development of the U.S. Capitol,[7] is a diagram of Indian villages in and around the city, which was based on the mapping that was done by Proudfit in the late 1800s. It includes the Native village site that Proudfit identified less than half a mile from the Capitol.[8]

As Proudfit also explained in his writings, when he found a spot that had assorted artifacts and included pottery, he concluded that it was not just a campground used temporarily by hunters but a site where food was prepared and constituted a village. Proudfit identified a number of village sites on the east bank of the Anacostia River, but only two on the west side, near the

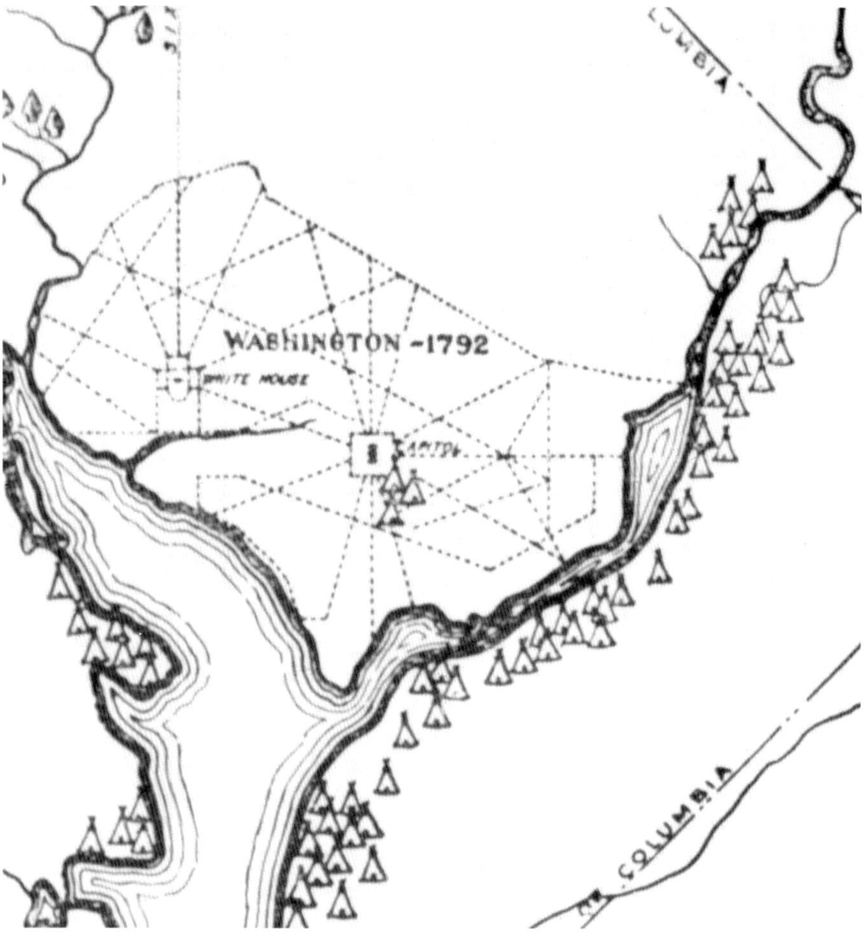

Diagram of Indian villages. *U.S. Government Printing Office, 1930, modified by author.*

center of the city. Even in the 1880s, the west side of the river was far more developed than the east side, so remains of additional villages on the west side may have been erased by development. (Proudfit's village sites will be discussed in more detail in chapters 2, 9 and 12.)

In the late 1880s, Proudfit inspected the grounds of the Daniel Carroll estate, before the site was cleared and housing built. Daniel Carroll had owned most of the land now called the Capitol Hill neighborhood, including the site where the Capitol now sits. His estate was nearby, built in 1790. Carroll lived there until his death in 1847, and his children occupied the house and the estate until the 1880s, when they decided to sell the site for redevelopment.

The grounds of the estate had never been substantially disturbed, and when Proudfit searched for artifacts on the estate, he found the variety that indicated it had once been a Native village.

When I found Proudfit's article on the village site near the Capitol and close to the nearby National Museum of the American Indian (NMAI), I put the information together and sent it to then Director of the NMAI, Kevin Gover, in July 2016.

My question then—which unfortunately is still an open question today—was, "Why are visitors to the NMAI not told about this Native site so close to the museum?"

This is one of many facets of the Native American history of Washington, DC, that is explored in the chapters that follow. The frustrations that have risen out of finding a rich assortment of Native artifacts, including the remains of Natives, around the city and seeing them unacknowledged in Washington have led me to blog and to assemble a website with a map to tell the stories under the auspices of a group now called the DC Native History Project.

Carroll family on manor porch. *Library of Congress, Prints and Photographs Division.*

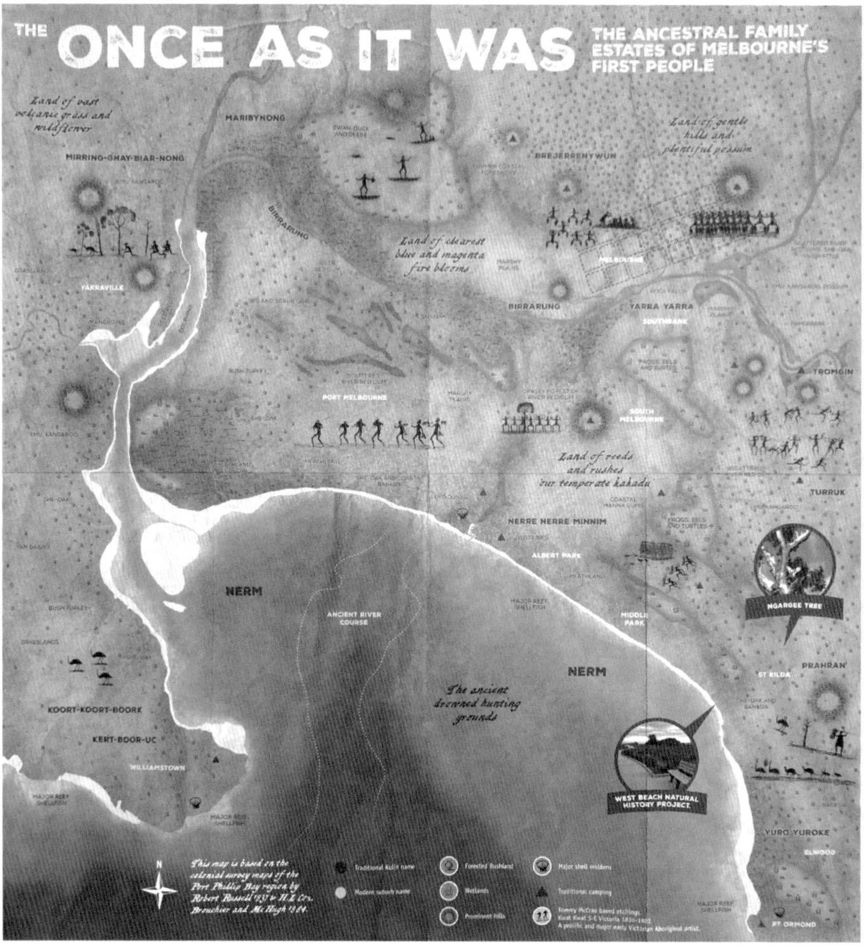

The *Once as It Was* map of Melbourne. Australia. *Map image used with the permission of the Boon Wurrung Foundation and the Port Phillip EcoCentre.*

As can be found online, the *Once As It Was Map of Washington, DC,*[9] was inspired by a map I found in 2018 in Melbourne, Australia, that was available in all their public libraries.

Using a base drawn from two Melbourne maps from the 1800s, the *Once As It Was Map of Melbourne* gives a graphic display of where the Indigenous People of Melbourne had lived before British settlers arrived in the 1830s. When I got back to DC in the spring of 2018, a search in the Geography and Maps Division of the Library of Congress located a 1790 topographic map of the land that was to become Washington.[10] Onto a revised version of that map, I added clickable icons that produce a pop-up page telling the stories of the many sites found around Washington. Also on the map is access to an unpublished article that explains the included sites in more detail and gives references for their source materials. Currently, the map contains nearly twenty icons with stories of DC's Native American history.

Before closing this preface, I should explain why my early work about the Native history of Washington neglected the important Palisades neighborhood on the northwest edge of the city. As is discussed in chapter 12, Proudfit considered this part of the city a major area for Native American life. But based on my initial experiences, if the documented finds near the Capitol, as well as the artifacts found on the White House lawn, could not get recognition in the city, the Native history of the Palisades neighborhood, which is far from the center of Washington, seemed unlikely to become a focus for public attention no matter how rich the finds. However, in my work to collect a fuller picture of the city's Native history to include in this book, I looked more closely at the important archaeological finds made in the Palisades and worked with several people and groups who live there to detail their rich history.

Introduction

This book collects and explains most of the available stories about the long history—several thousand years—of Native American life on the land that is now Washington, DC. Whenever possible, it relates the stories of the tribe that lived on the land, the Anacostans, when the English settlers arrived in the 1600s. The stories are set in such central locations as the lawn of the White House and within a few blocks of the Capitol, but they also range widely across the city—up through Rock Creek Park and to the northwest corner of Washington.

The sources of the stories range from detailed archaeological digs—like the work that was done in 1997 before a highway ramp was built on the edge of the Foggy Bottom neighborhood and nineteenth-century research in the quarries near Rock Creek—to news reports that managed to get space in nineteenth-century dailies, when the city was being built. The oldest news report dates to 1866 (see chapter 10). The most recent major find was reported in a detailed paper in 2009 (see chapter 11). In neighborhoods like the Palisades, in northwest DC, people are finding artifacts on their property almost daily (see chapter 12).

In addition to telling those stories, the epilogue for this book discusses where they should be told—on the streets and in the cultural institutions and museums of Washington—and tries to explain why they are not readily available to the adults and children of the city and its many national visitors. That discussion also includes possible ways DC residents and visitors can help get Native American history to be a central part of the life of this city.

1

How Did the Anacostans Get Their Name?

Mistakes Were Made

The first contact between English settlers and the Anacostan Natives of Washington, DC, happened in 1608, when Captain John Smith and his crew sailed up the Potomac from Jamestown in Virginia. Captain Smith was only twenty-eight years old at the time.[11] His adventurous career that brought him to Jamestown at this early age had begun when he was sixteen and became a soldier, fighting the Spanish in France and the Netherlands for two years.[12] At age twenty, he set off for Austria to join the Christian armies fighting the wars with the Muslim Ottoman Turks. During his rambling journey to Austria, Smith joined the crew of a pirate ship in the Mediterranean and earned a bounty of five hundred gold pieces to pay for the rest of his remaining travels. In Austria, he joined the army of the Holy Roman Empire and fought against the Turks in battles waged in Slovenia, Hungary and Transylvania (now Romania), earning several awards for his bravery in battle. One award was his promotion to captain, a title young Smith wore prominently for the rest of his life.

In 1602, Smith was wounded, captured and sold into slavery in the Ottoman Empire. This extended his travels to Constantinople, where he lived as a poorly treated slave until he overpowered and killed his cruel master, stealing his horse to escape. This involved him traveling through parts of Russia, Ukraine, Germany, France, Spain and Morocco and returning to England in 1604.

In London, Smith learned of plans to establish a colony in the New World. This colony would be located in the central part of the east coast

Captain John Smith. *Library of Congress, Prints and Photographs Division.*

of the sprawling area from what we now know as Maine to the Carolinas, which would eventually be the home of thirteen British colonies. In 1585, Sir Walter Raleigh had been granted permission to colonize in the central area of the coast by Queen Elizabeth.[13] He named the area "Virginia." in honor of his "Virgin Queen," Elizabeth I.

In the late 1500s, a group of colonizers sponsored by Raleigh and some other wealthy Englishmen had tried to establish themselves on Roanoke Island, off the coast of what is now North Carolina. That colony was left without support from England for nearly three years, and no survivors were found when John White, their former leader, returned to look for them in 1590.[14]

The new Virginia Company was chartered by King James I on April 10, 1606. Smith's military exploits impressed the men who organized the Virginia Company. Despite being the youngest of the colonizers, he was given a position as one of the leaders. In December 1606, three ships carrying 104 men, including Smith, left London, sailed to the Canary Islands and Puerto Rico for supplies and arrived at the site that would become Jamestown in May 1607.[15]

Initially, Smith was put in charge of procuring goods and supplies from the local environment and the Native Americans. Infighting among the other leaders of the colony led to Smith becoming the official leader of the colony in 1608.[16]

The land the colonizers had chosen for their fort and town was part of the domain of Chief Powhatan. In December 1607, when Smith was searching for food along a nearby river, he was captured by Chief Powhatan's men and brought to meet with the chief. This first encounter with Chief Powhatan, the supreme leader over a number of tribes in the Chesapeake region, was the basis for the tale of Pocahontas saving Smith's life. Historians have cast doubt on whether the captain's life was really saved by Powhatan's favorite daughter, Pocahontas, who was only twelve years old at the time.[17] Smith only reported that story years later, when writing to the queen to speak favorably of Pocahontas after she migrated to England.

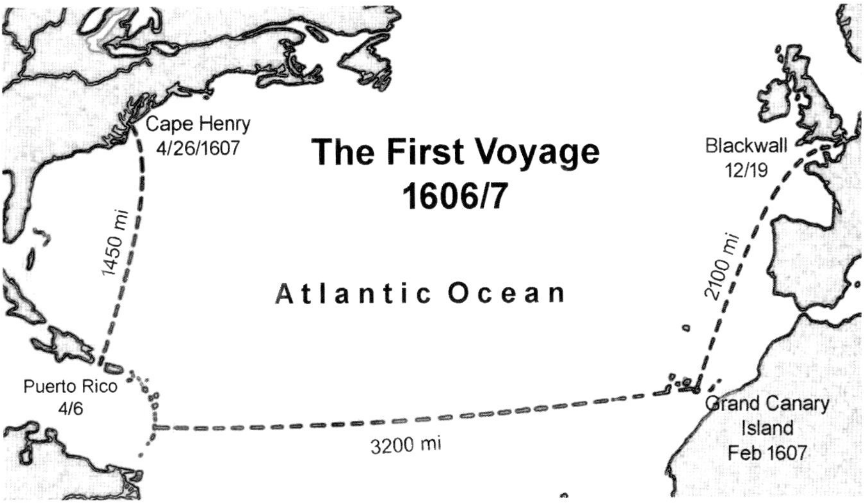

First settler voyage to Jamestown. *Drawn by author. Base map courtesy of Library of Congress, Geography and Map Division.*

We know Powhatan released Smith, and relations between the chief and the colony remained unsettled during and after the reign of Powhatan, which contributed to the troubles and starvation the colonizers were to experience during their first years in Jamestown.

In June 1608, Smith left Jamestown to explore the Chesapeake Bay region and search for badly needed food. Powhatan had sent out word to tribes under his influence not to cooperate with Smith and his crew, and Smith reported that he did not find friendly tribes until he traveled to the northern part of the Potomac.[18] This was an area dominated by the Piscataway tribe, which was not friendly with Powhatan.

Among his crew, Captain Smith had mapmakers who tried to collect the name of the tribes they encountered and record their village locations for a map they were making. When Smith and his crew got to the area where the Joint Base Anacostia-Bolling now sits, they labeled the Piscataway tribe they found there "Nacotchtanck."

The proximity of this tribe to the confluence of a second river that joined with the Potomac (now the Anacostia) put them in a choice location to be traders, and the name Nacotchtanck was meant to mean "a town of traders."

Although there isn't a clear record for it, Smith may have welcomed the chance to trade for food from this tribe. Smith sailed back to Jamestown and was officially made leader of the colony in September 1608. In October 1609, Smith was injured in a gunpowder explosion and returned to England.

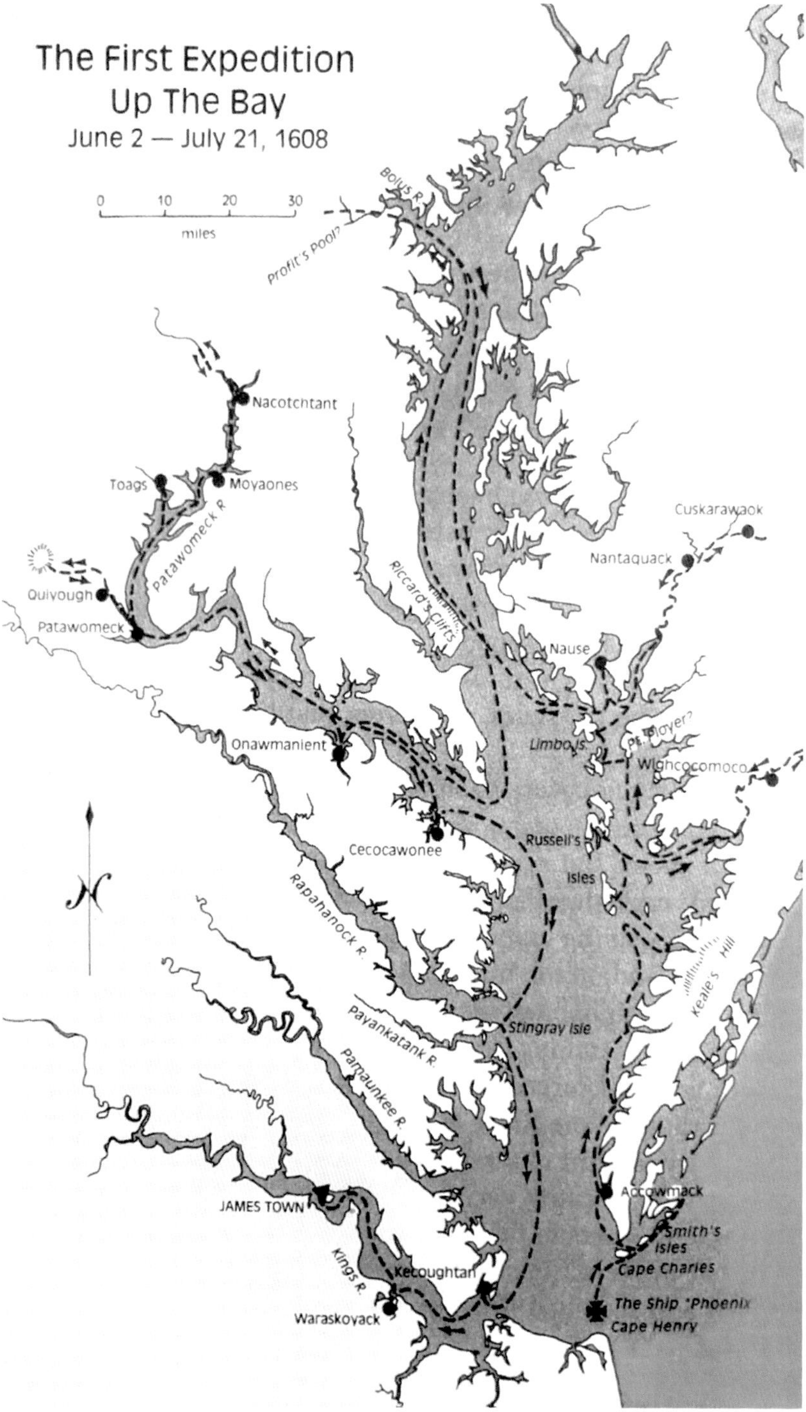
The First Expedition
Up The Bay
June 2 — July 21, 1608
0 10 20 30
miles
Bolus R.
Profit's Pool?
Nacotchtant
Toags
Moyaones
Patawomeck R.
Quiyough
Patawomeck
Riccard's Cliffs
Cuskarawaok
Nantaquack
Nause
Limbo Is.
Pt. Ployer?
Wighcocomoco
Onawmanient
Cecocawonee
Russell's
Isles
Rapahanock R.
Keale's Hill
Stingray Isle
Payankatank R.
Pamaunkee R.
JAMES TOWN
Kings R.
Kecoughtan
Waraskoyack
Accowmack
Smith's
Isles
Cape Charles
The Ship "Phoenix
Cape Henry

Opposite: First Smith Expedition around the Chesapeake Bay. *Haile, E.W. Roundhouse, Champlain, Virginia.*

Above: John Smith map 1612 with Nacotchtanck enlarged. *Library of Congress, Geography and Map Division, modified by author.*

Smith's map of the Chesapeake was published in 1612.[19] But within a little more than twenty years after the publication of Smith's map, the name for the tribe was changed by a prominent settler who had studied the language of the Piscataways. That settler was the Jesuit priest, Father Andrew White, who came to the colonies in 1634 to convert the Natives to Christianity. In order to preach to the Natives, White studied the local Piscataway dialect of the Algonquin language. Various forms of Algonquin were used by Native American tribes on the East Coast of North America and even tribes farther inland.

Father White changed the map name "Nacotchtanck" used for the tribe of traders by adding an *a* sound to the beginning of the name. From his understanding of the language, he noticed, as have other commentators after him,[20] that the word for "a town of traders," would be "anaquashatanik." This word is based on the two Algonquin words *anaquash*, meaning "to trade," and *tanik*, signifying a town.

Public interest in the Native tribe of DC often starts with reference to Captain Smith's 1608 map, and it isn't hard to find citations online with the name "Nacotchtanck" or a variation of that name, including an entry on Wikipedia.[21]

The 1894 article by Tooker[22] points out that Captain Smith never used the spelling "Nacotchtanck" from his map when he wrote about the tribe. He did use five other names: Nacotchtanke, Nacothtant, Nacotchtant, Nacotchtanks and Necosts.

The Wikipedia description of the origin of the Anacostan name seems to come from this statement by James Mooney in a collection of 1899 articles on the First People of DC that also included the work of S.V. Proudfit: "Nacochtank, which was the residence of a chief and contained eighty warriors, was the principal settlement within or adjoining the District. The Jesuits, who came out later with Lord Baltimore, latinized the name as Anacostan."[23] Mooney's linguistic studies involved the Native languages of the Southwest, not Piscataway or other Algonquin languages. The one Jesuit who changed the name was Andrew White, described above. "Latinizing" the name was not his goal.

In the early 1790s, when Thomas Jefferson was secretary of state, he asked Andrew Ellicott to investigate the Native American name for the "Eastern Branch" of the Potomac. The historical record is not clear, but Ellicott found the name to be "Annakostia." Jefferson encouraged him to use it, and Ellicott did include the name on his 1793 map of the "Territory of Columbia."[24]

The errors in the spellings of the original name aren't surprising. Since Algonquin languages do not have an alphabet, Smith's mapmakers couldn't just ask, "How do you spell that?" Variations on the names of Native tribes are common. A 1787 document on the transcription of Native American languages by English settlers includes this comment: "Almost every man who writes Indian words, spells them in a peculiar manner."[25]

The new name introduced by Father White led to several variations for the name among the other English settlers, but one of the most popular derivative forms became "Anacostan." As evidence that the Nacotchtanck name was rapidly replaced by forms similar to Anacostan, the 1666 Articles of Peace and Amity that were established between Lord Calvert and several Native tribes does not include Nacotchtanck but lists the tribe as "Anacostanck."[26]

Since the name Anacostia refers to a major neighborhood and river in Washington, DC, referring to its Native tribe as the Anacostans pulls together these names and helps listeners understand their association.

A 1793 map of "Territory of Columbia," by Andrew Ellicott showing "Annakostia" river name. *Library of Congress, Geography and Map Division.*

The Native Americans weren't the only foreign group who got their names mangled by local English speakers. For example, the Amish people, who migrated from Germany and settled in Pennsylvania in the mid-1700s, would have told English speakers that they were German by saying they were "Deutsch." That was taken by the English to mean they were Dutch, and now the Amish are commonly referred to as the "Pennsylvania Dutch."

So, the name Nacotchtank and variations still get used by many people, laymen and scholars, who start with the John Smith map as a reference. But that map's mistake should not be the basis for naming the Piscataway tribe that once lived in Washington, DC. They were a tribe of traders and are more correctly called the Anacostans.[27]

2

The Native Village Five Blocks from the U.S. Capitol

Garfield Park History

The construction of Garfield Park began in 1883 on a piece of land in southeast Washington, DC. Labeled as Reservation No. 17, it was set aside for a park in Pierre L'Enfant's original city plan. The park was named for President James Garfield after his assassination in 1881.

James Garfield was elected president just two hundred days before he died of infectious complications from a gunshot wound he received on July 2, 1881. He was shot by Charles J. Guiteau, an embittered attorney, in the central Washington railroad station—now the location of the main building of the National Gallery of Art, on the National Mall.

After being shot, Garfield lived for a little more than two months. To get away from the summer heat of Washington, Garfield was moved by train to his home in New Jersey in early September. He died there on September 19, 1881. One of Garfield's attending physicians, and an old friend of the president, was Colonel Almon Rockwell. In an odd coincidence, Rockwell was also one of the attending physicians on the night Lincoln died.

Even before President Garfield took office, he had arranged for Rockwell to be superintendent of public buildings for Washington, DC.[28] In that role, Rockwell oversaw the construction of the park built to honor his friend, the fallen president. The people of Washington seemed to know Rockwell well enough that one of the two newspaper articles reporting on the Native American artifacts found when the park was built described him only by saying, "The laborers under Colonel Rockwell," without additional

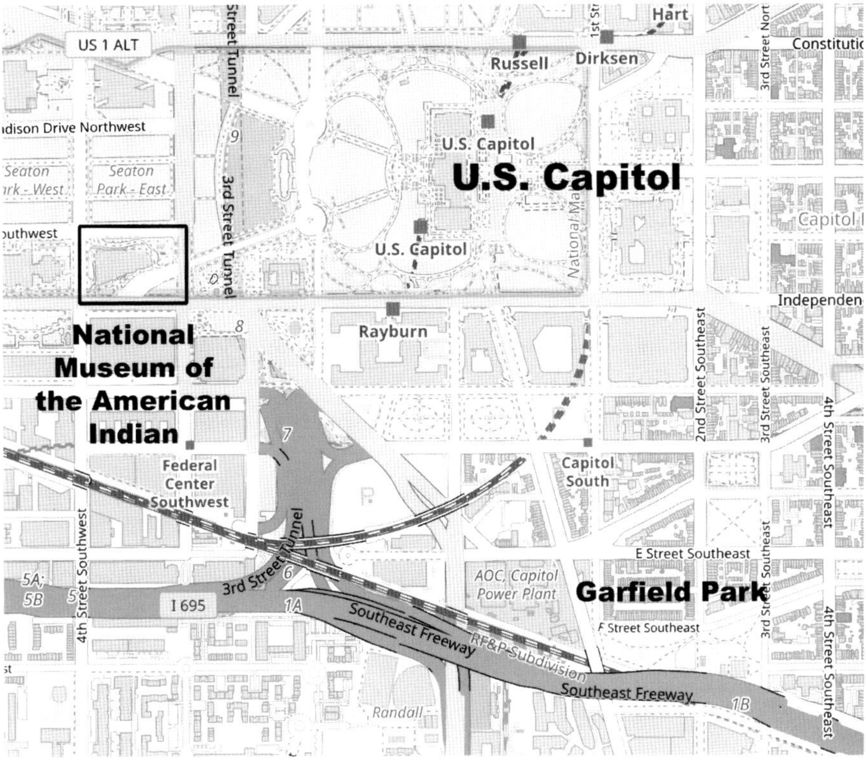

Map of Garfield Park and area near Capitol. *Open Street Maps.*

comment on who he was.[29] A second news report, from the *Washington Post*, is a more rambling piece,[30] written in the loose newspaper style of the late 1880s, where people interviewed aren't clearly identified.

The major Native American artifacts described in both articles are a wooden stake that appeared to once have been used to hold canoes on the edge of a body of water and some bones of what was later identified as a young girl. Also found was "hair straight and black, like that of Indians."[31]

In archaeology, hair can be a valuable source of clues about the subject under study. However, since degradation of hair is affected by many environmental factors after death, it is not used to judge the age of the findings. In the case of the Garfield Park remains, the description of the hair indicates it was from a Native American and not a more recent burial by English settlers. In contrast, the description of a child's shoe that was found, "of a very old fashion," could have been lost by one the children that had grown up on the Carroll estate, which had sat on the land next to the park since the 1790s.

James Garfield assassination. *From* Frank Leslie's Illustrated Newspaper, *July 16, 1881; Library of Congress, Prints and Photographs Division.*

The Identification of the Village Site by Samuel Vincent Proudfit

Garfield Park as a historic Native American site was first identified by nineteenth-century archaeologist Samuel Vincent Proudfit. Proudfit was a rather private man. Much of our information on his life and work, outside of his archaeological publications, must be assembled indirectly, since he seems to have avoided the sort of historic coverage of many of his peers.

The clues to Proudfit's involvement in the story of the Garfield Park artifacts are part of the *Washington Post* report on the artifacts.[32] In the story, the reporter interviews an unidentified "superintendent of reservation No. 17." As mentioned earlier, Reservation No. 17 was Pierre L'Enfant's original name for the Garfield Park site. When the park was being built, it was federal land that would be overseen by the U.S. Department of the Interior (DOI).

The chief clue in that story that suggests the "superintendent" was Proudfit is a reference to his work in Missouri regarding petrified materials. In this news article, the superintendent notes that the found materials were some that "I have found myself." Before moving to Washington, DC, to

Garfield Park map with historic Carroll Estate. *Library of Congress, Geography and Map Division.*

work as an attorney on land disputes for the DOI, Proudfit worked in the St. Louis office and did research on the many precolonial Native American mounds that had been left in and around St. Louis.[33] This clue that Proudfit was involved in the artifacts found in 1883 in Garfield Park helps explain why he was interested in studying the grounds of the adjoining Carroll estate in 1886 before it was cleared for new construction.

Proudfit's Examination of the Carroll Estate

In the late 1700s, Daniel Carroll of Duddington inherited a large tract of land in what was to become the city of Washington, DC, from his father, Charles Carroll. The Carrolls were an influential family in the area and included Daniel Carroll's second cousin Charles Carroll of Carrollton (1737–1832), a signer of the Declaration of Independence.

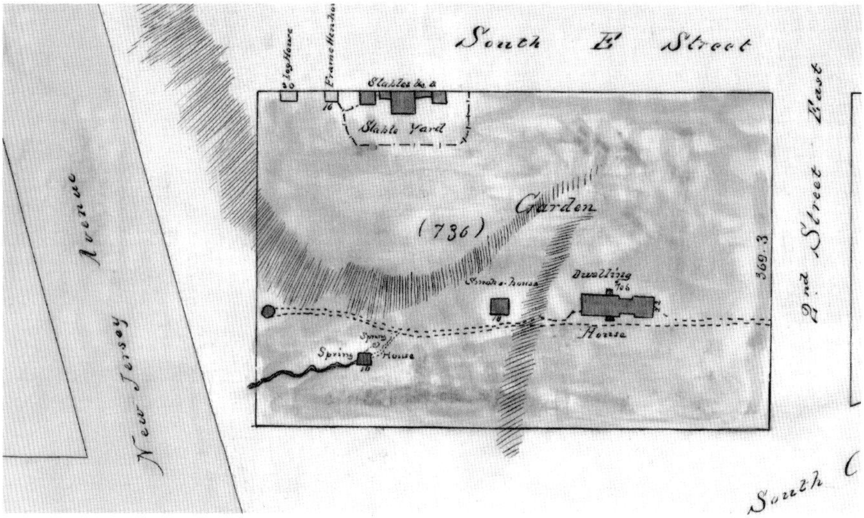

Carroll Estate showing New Jersey Avenue. *Library of Congress, Geography and Map Division.*

In 1791, Daniel Carroll started construction of his estate within an area L'Enfant had designated as the path of New Jersey Avenue. Because it conflicted with his street plan, L'Enfant sent in men and demolished what had been built. This outraged Carroll and the city commissioners (one of which was Daniel Carroll of Rock Creek, a second cousin) and resulted in the dismissal of L'Enfant from his role as a designer of Washington.[34] The second site Carroll used for his estate (L'Enfant's Square 736) is just east of the original site and now sits near New Jersey Avenue, SE.

A search at the Library of Congress Geography and Map Division for Square 736 brings up a detailed map of the Carroll Estate. That map shows that the estate was built around a spring, which made it attractive to Carroll. The spring would have provided an important source of fresh water for the Native Americans who lived there in the past.

Proudfit used "village" in the title of his major publication that described the Carroll Estate.[35] This drawing by John White of an Algonquin "village" from the 1700s shows how the Natives sometimes collected in a fortified space, probably during times of conflict with other tribes. But Proudfit repeatedly clarified how he used the term *village*, because such clustered living was not typical for local Native Americans:

> *It should be remembered that an Indian village of the Potomac was not a compact assemblage of houses, but scattered dwellings along a watercourse,*

Daniel Carroll Manor. *Library of Congress, Prints and Photographs Division.*

Town of Pomeiock, John White drawing. Note the dog shown in the upper left of the village. *Library of Congress, Prints and Photographs Division.*

> *with the intervening spaces usually under cultivation. In some instances, however, a cluster of houses might be found at such points as afforded more than the ordinary riparian advantages, but usually the dwellings were comparatively isolated.*[36]

When not under attack, Algonquin Natives lived in open or dispersed towns, where families would cluster a few wigwams and farm nearby, with some space between groups.[37]

Proudfit also clarified how he decided to classify a site as a place where Native families had lived, as compared with the temporary hunting sites that he had also encountered:

> *An examination of any cultivated field that lies along the Potomac or Anacostia will furnish more or less evidence of temporary occupation. The difference between these places and village sites is readily discernible in the character of the remains, as well as in the quantity. The former show flakes, and chips of stone, with here and there an implement of the knife and arrowhead type, while the latter, with its ever-present pottery, seems to have left its mark on every stone in the field. The wreck of an old village can never be mistaken for the campground of a single season.*[38]

With a map of the estate and a description Proudfit gave in one of his papers,[39] we can roughly pinpoint the area where he found most of the artifacts on the Carroll estate:

> *This was the old Carroll Place, and at the time of my visit in 1889, it was unoccupied and the streets had recently been graded, leaving the old mansion with its surrounding grounds at the old level. The bank exposure thus resulting on the west side showed undisputed evidence of an old village site from which I collected a number of specimens of flint and pottery.*

Proudfit found an assortment of stone points and pottery on the Carroll site when he inspected it. Unfortunately, the records he left of his finds don't allow us to pinpoint specific items. Late in his life, Proudfit donated his journal with records of his finds to the National Museum (now the Smithsonian Institution). The journal can be inspected online,[40] and it shows that Proudfit had an odd style for labeling his entries. Page after page in his journal detail that much of his collecting was done in the Benning Road area on the east bank of the Anacostia. A few other sites are labeled with

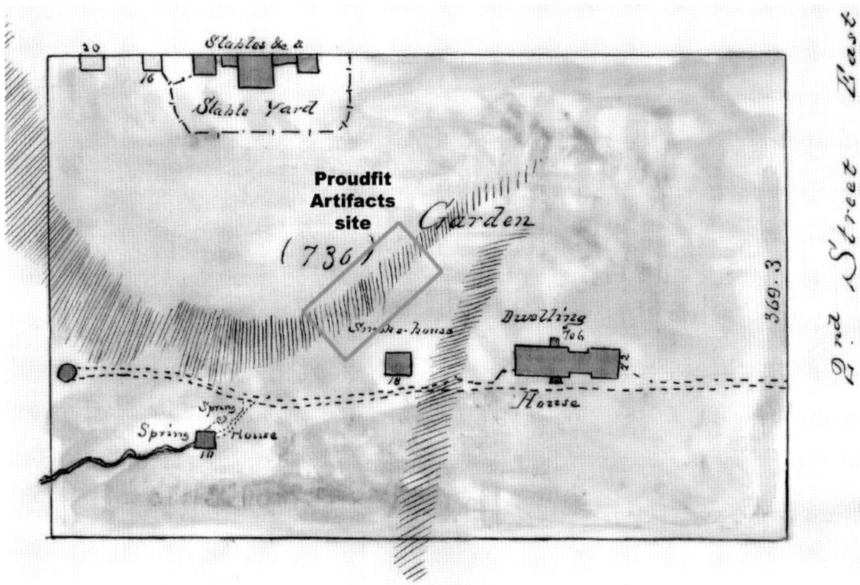

Carroll Estate map with area of artifact finds marked. *Library of Congress, Geography and Map Division, modified by author.*

specific names, but most are just labeled "District of Columbia." None are labeled for the Carroll estate or the second village site he identified on what is now the U.S. National Arboretum (see chapter 8). Of course, the Benning Road area is also part of the District of Columbia, but it seems Proudfit had a classification system in mind that divided the District into either Benning Road or the rest of the city.

Although we can't identify the specific artifacts from the Carroll Estate, we have records and images of Proudfit's large collection of artifacts from Washington, DC. We know from his writings that the artifacts included stone points, blades and pottery. A detailed analysis of the time periods represented by the finds for the Native American history of Washington is not possible, but the reality of the finds is indisputable.

3

The Anacostans and Their Dogs

Many of the current residents of Capitol Hill know Garfield Park as a place where they and their neighbors walk their dogs. From what we know about the local Native Americans who once lived on that land, it's likely that they once ran their dogs on the same land that is now the park.

An important part of what we know about the Algonquin Natives of the mid-Atlantic region—which includes the Anacostans of DC—can be indirectly traced back to Sir Walter Raleigh, the sixteenth-century soldier and explorer. Raleigh promoted exploration and settlement in the mid-Atlantic in the late 1500s. In 1585, he sent his cousin Sir Richard Grenville and an artist-mapmaker, John White, to explore the area that is now North Carolina.

In 1586, Raleigh organized a group of 113 settlers to travel once again to the "New World" and establish a colony.[41] This time, Raleigh chose John White as its leader. The settlers left England on May 8, 1587, and a group of them landed on Roanoke Island, as part of what is now Virginia, in July to establish a colony. Among the settlers was John White's pregnant daughter, Eleanor, and her husband, Ananias Dare. One month after they arrived, Eleanor gave birth to the first colonist born in their New World. She was named Virginia.

Arriving in late summer, the settlers quickly realized that they would not be able to grow crops before winter, so John White was dispatched to England for supplies. He left only ten days after his granddaughter was born.[42]

Tragically for White and the settlers, when he returned to England, war with Spain led Queen Elizabeth I to forbid any ship to be used for nonmilitary missions. It would be three years before he would be able to return to Roanoke Island. When White did return, the site was abandoned. The mystery of what happened to the "Lost Colony" is still debated today. White returned to England, disheartened, and never sailed to the Americas again.

Fortunately for our understanding of Native life, White produced several watercolor paintings of what he had seen during his two visits to America. These paintings provide our best records of what Algonquin Natives looked like and how they lived before the influences of the settlers.

One of White's drawings is the town of Pomeiock, shown in the previous chapter. In the upper left, he included a dog. The dog portrayed is relatively small, about knee height. In archaeological studies, solid details about the size of Native dogs have come from measurements made on the bones of canines found buried in single graves or in graves with human remains.[43]

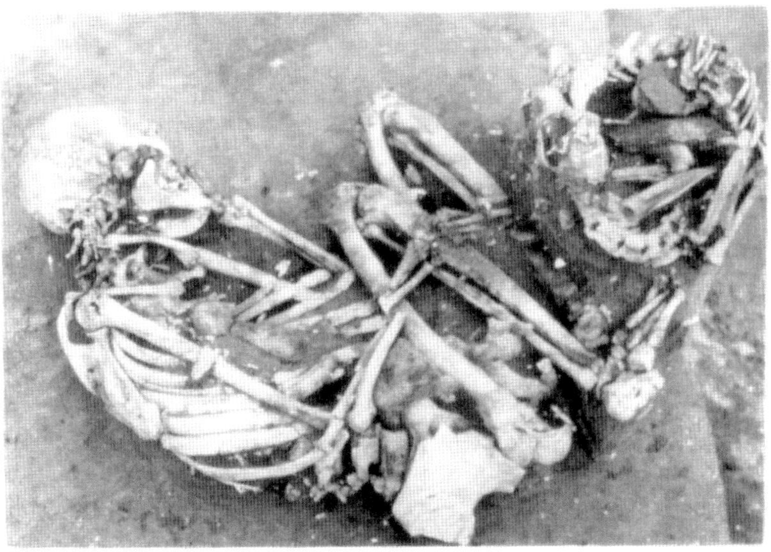

Figure 2. Feature A168 at Weyanoke Old Town contained the remains of an elderly female (HBA2) with a dog (DBA23) buried over the top of her feet and covered with a whole pot or potsherds from the same Late Woodland vessel (sherds removed for photograph). Excavated and photographed by the author and D. Scott Speedy, October 1985.

Dog buried with Native Woman at Weyanoke site. *JP Blick and DS Speedy, Algonquian Papers, 2000.*

Those measurements show that the Native dogs were of medium size and probably weighed between forty and sixty pounds.

White's drawing that shows a dog in the Native village indicates that dogs were found among the Natives in their daily life. Clues about the value that the Algonquins put on their dogs have come from the study of numerous dog burials found around various Algonquin villages. A study of dog burials at one site near Weyanoke, which is about twenty-five miles from Colonial Williamsburg, Virginia, found the remains of 112 dogs.[44] An important find at that site also showed that dogs were sometimes buried with Natives.

Not all Native people in the Americas treated dogs with such respect. Among ancient people who commonly considered dogs as a food source, dog bones are typically found in heaps of debris mixed with the bones of other animals. There was no evidence of dogs being eaten in the archaeological study of Weyanoke.

Among the Algonquins, it's likely that dogs were used for hunting.[45] Based on their size and some comments made by early settlers, they would have been used to hunt "land fowl," such as turkeys, and small game, like rabbits, squirrels and racoons. The extent to which they were kept as pets must be left to speculation. However, the friendly nature of many canines makes it likely that some human-dog bonding occurred, and the burial shown in the picture on the previous page does document at least one such case.

WHERE DID THE NATIVE DOGS ORIGINATE?

Until the 1970s, it was assumed that the Natives of North America had domesticated their dogs from wolves, as was done by various cultures around the world. A new theory was introduced during the 1970s by Dr. I. Lehr Brisbin, a biologist and former researcher at the University of Georgia.[46] During Brisbin's work studying the ecology of the Savannah River on the South Carolina border, he began observing the packs of wild dogs in the local fields and swamps. He noticed that they looked like the Australian dingo and other dogs found in southeast Asia. Brisbin was the first to suggest that the dogs now found wild in the American South and the dogs found as far away as Australia may have all been descended from a common breed that once lived in Siberia. Dr. Brisbin named the wild dogs he saw the Carolina Dog, and he became a major public advocate of the Carolina Dog (also called the "Dixie Dingo"). His efforts got the Carolina Dog recognized in

A Carolina Dog. *Wikipedia Commons.*

1995 as a standard breed by the American Kennel Club and the American Rare Breed Association.[47]

However, it wasn't until 2012 that the application of new forms of genetic analysis provided proof that there was a genetic link between Carolina Dogs and breeds from Siberia.[48] The technique used an analysis of the unique DNA found in mitochondria. The researchers noted that among the many breeds they analyzed, their data clearly supported an ancient Asian origin of the Carolina Dog.

As an indirect, visual support for the link between the Carolina Dog and those that lived with the Algonquin Natives in the mid-Atlantic is the similarity of the outline of the dog seen in the John White drawing with a photo of a Carolina Dog. Considering both visual and genetic evidence, it appears that the ancestors of the Carolina Dog may have migrated with the people who moved from the Asian land mass into North America over nine thousand years ago.[49]

Released in the summer of 2022, the science fiction movie *Prey* includes a Carolina Dog, Coco, as the helper of a Comanche woman who hunts and eventually (spoiler alert) kills an alien Predator threatening her tribe. The Comanches respected and kept dogs, but based on reports that they allowed wolves to mate with their dogs[50] and the use of dogs to pull travois holding tribe goods across the Plains, it seems likely that Comanche dogs were bigger than the East Coast Carolina Dog. Despite this possible bit of canine miscasting, the strong Native American cast and Coco, the Carolina Dog, made this film an excellent addition to the Predator film franchise.

Considering our various records that relate to the dogs of the Anacostans and the Algonquins, the modern dog walkers of Garfield Park apparently share a common bond with canines and the Native Americans who previously walked that land.

4

The Native American Quarries in Northwest Washington, DC

Working stone to make tools, weapons, pipes and bowls was a fundamental part of Native American life. The Anacostans and the tribes that preceded them in this area for several thousand years worked stone from two major quarries. Both quarries were in what is now the northwest of the city and parts of Rock Creek Park.

The Piney Branch Quartzite Quarry

Making a stone tool that has an edge for cutting or piercing can only be done with a few types of stone. Flint is a sedimentary form of quartz that readily breaks into sharp-edged pieces. But flint is not commonly found in the mid-Atlantic region, and the largest source of flint for the local Natives was about four hundred miles away, in what is now Ohio.

A common local stone that was used for tool and weapon-making was quartzite. Although quartzite is not as easy to work as flint, its availability made it widely used for arrowheads, blades and a variety of other items.

In 1889, William Henry Holmes began his intensive study of the quartzite quarry that was located near where the Piney Branch Creek crossed 14th Street Road, NW, which would later correspond to what is now 16th Street, NW.

In July 1889, Holmes took a new job as an archaeologist in the U.S. Bureau of Ethnology, which later became part of the Smithsonian

Left: Flint. *Wikipedia Commons.*

Right: Quartzite cobble and split cobble showing edge. *Photo by author.*

Department of Anthropology. As he noted in his key 1890 paper on the Piney Branch quarry:

> *I resolved to commence work at home—literally at home—for the nearest site in which these rude implements are found, and one of the most promising sites for archaeologic research in the United States, was only one and a quarter miles from my own doorstep in this city.*[51]

Holmes had seen previous references to the quarry made by Proudfit and others, but he didn't feel it had been adequately studied. During the time Holmes did his work, the Piney Branch Creek extended up to 14th Street, NW. Later development of 16th Street, NW, would fill in the creek bed farther west. At the original site, Holmes described the slopes of the creek rising about one hundred feet above the water and, to a naive viewer, just hillsides with a number of cobblestones.

It was Holmes's work that identified and measured the great piles of debris that had been left by Native Americans when they worked stone there. His work showed how extensively the site had been used to collect and work with quartzite for centuries.[52]

Working stone is not a simple or reliable process. A chosen stone is hit and cracked. This process is called knapping. Knapping is the process of chipping away pieces of a larger stone to shape a tool or stone point. The word originates from the German *knopp*, meaning "to strike, shape or work." If the first crack looks promising, the artisan continues, hoping to

Right: William Henry Holmes. *Library of Congress, Prints and Photographs Division.*

Below: An 1884 topographic map of Washington, DC, showing future extension of 16th Street NW across Piney Branch Valley. *Library of Congress, Geography and Map Division, modified by author.*

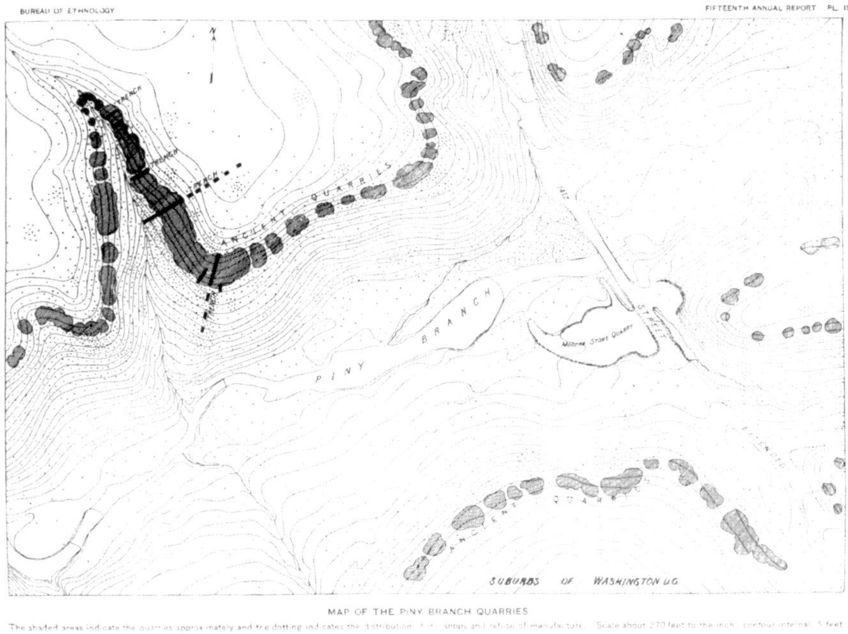

Above: Map of Piney Branch Quarries. *W.H. Holmes, 1897. Google Books.*

Right: W.H. Holmes at Piney Branch quarry. *Smithsonian Institution.*

Quartzite quarry samples arranged to show blade production. *National Park Service.*

shape the stone into an arrowhead or cutting tool. Often, the chosen stone fails to become a finished object. Stone working produces a lot more debris than successes.

In his work at the quarry, Holmes dug trenches to get an estimate of the size of the debris field left by Natives who had worked there. He found a belt of worked material fifty-five feet wide and upward of six feet deep. Holmes estimated that the debris belt might extend half a mile or more. Overall, it was clear that the site had been worked for hundreds or even thousands of years. He did not find any clues to distinguish differences between the various groups that had worked the site. It was conjecture on his part, but he suggested that this quarry was the chief source of the quartzite implements found at various Native sites around Washington, DC.

Holmes's proposed statue for the Piney Branch quarry. *Smithsonian Institution.*

To show what the process of knapping quartzite might look like when a sample was refined into a finish form, Holmes included representative samples from his collections in the preceding illustration.

Holmes was struck by how extensive the quartzite remains were at the quarry and throughout the area:

> *So numerous, indeed, are these objects in certain localities that they are brought in with every load of gravel from the creek beds, and the laborer who sits by the way-side breaking bowlders for our streets each year passes them by thousands beneath his hammer; and it is literally true that this city, the capital of a civilized nation, is paved with the art remains of a race who occupied its site in the shadowy past.*[53]

Because of his extensive work as an illustrator and painter, when Holmes was in his seventies, he was appointed director of the newly formed National Gallery of Art. In his personal papers, there is an account of a 1925 visit Holmes paid to the Piney Branch quarry site with the city engineer, where they discussed erecting at the site a bronze sculpture that Holmes had modeled in clay. He hoped that the sculpture would serve as a monument to the Native people who had worked in the quarry and be a beautiful embellishment to the park. The monument was never built.

THE ROSE HILL SOAPSTONE QUARRY

Soapstone, technically called steatite, is a light-colored rock composed of the clay mineral talc. Some samples have a soft finish making them feel like soap, which gives the stone its name.

Soapstone is easy to carve, and it has been used in many cultures around the world, including Native Americans. The use of this stone to make pots has given it the alternate name potstone. It was also used to make bowls, other types of cooking vessels and tobacco pipes.

The major soapstone quarry in Washington, DC, was located on what is now the west side of Connecticut Avenue, NW, just above the campus of the University of the District of Columbia. The quarry was filled in the early twentieth century and is now the site of commercial buildings along Connecticut Avenue, below Albemarle Street, NW.

The walls around the quarry were described by Holmes as towering about eighty feet above the stream on the south side and about ten feet higher

Soapstone. *Photo by author.*

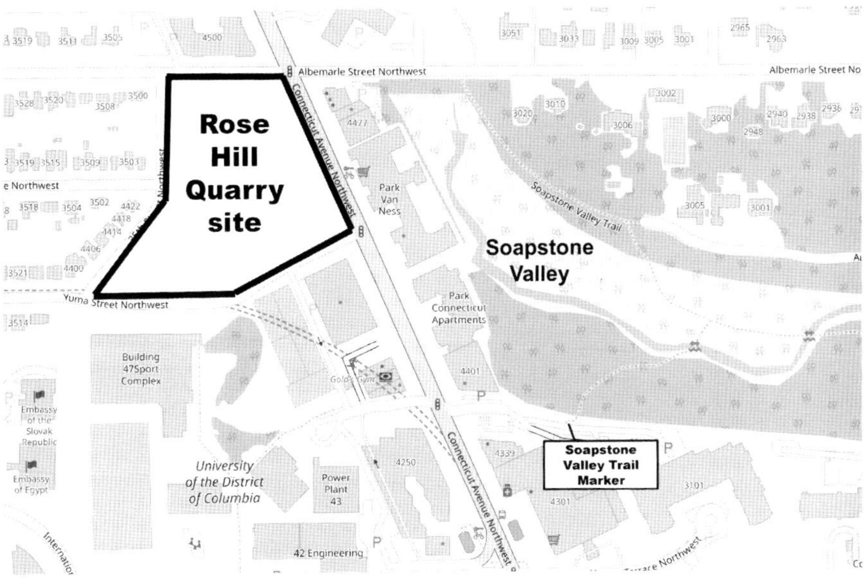

Map of Rose Hill Quarry site. *Open Street Maps, modified by author.*

on the north side.[54] In a ridge above the south side, the stone was exposed. When Holmes studied the quarry in the late 1880s, there was also evidence that settlers had quarried there. Even today, soapstone is quarried for use in products like countertops.

This quarry was first discovered in 1874 by Elmer R. Reynolds, an amateur archaeologist and botanist, who worked in Washington as an examiner of government pensions. As he described it: "In the summer of 1874…it was my good fortune during a half-aimless stroll, to stumble upon a curiously shaped, moss covered stone which, upon examination, proved to be a fragment of a soapstone mortar."[55]

Looking further in the area, Reynolds found the quarry site and later brought in a number of other interested archaeologists who had studied soapstone quarries around the United States. To them, this quarry appeared to be one of the choicest archaeological quarry sites in the country.[56] Reynolds collected several worked soapstone fragments and donated them to the Peabody Museum at Harvard University. Many of them can now be viewed online.[57]

Based on the soapstone artifacts found at the site, both Reynolds and Holmes concluded that, usually, the stone was roughly cut at the quarry and transported to other sites to be completed.

Most of the fragments found by Reynolds were oblong dishes, with handles of about an inch in length at each end. The image shown here is a drawing

Unfinished Soapstone bowl. *Drawing by Robert L. Humphrey, George Washington University.*

Soapstone Valley creek showing soapstone boulders in foreground. *Photo by author.*

of what a complete soapstone pot would look like. These stone pots could be put over a fire, roughly like our modern glass pans that are used for cooking in ovens.

As mentioned previously, the quarry was filled in the early twentieth century, and no signs of it remain. However, Soapstone Valley, which is on the east side of Connecticut Avenue, still connects the area to Rock Creek and remains a preserve for some of the quarry's history. The vestiges of the stream that once ran through the quarry still flow down Soapstone Valley, and there is a marked trail along the stream for visitors.

Soapstone Valley trail marker. *Photo by author.*

The National Park Service (NPS) oversees the streambed and the remains of the soapstone quarry. In the bed of that stream, visitors can inspect many pieces of soapstone. Removing any artifacts from the streambed is forbidden by NPS rules. Once again, it must be noted, there are no historical markers or other signage that explains the long history of the soapstone quarried and used by Natives Americans.

5

The Native American Artifacts Found on the White House Grounds in the 1970s

The story of the Native artifacts found on the White House (WH) grounds involves the construction of a swimming pool. The story of swimming pools at the WH began in 1933 when a pool was constructed in the West Wing for President Franklin Roosevelt.

In 1921, when he was thirty-nine years old, Roosevelt contracted polio, and his legs became permanently paralyzed. This led to him becoming an avid swimmer. His WH swimming pool was built soon after he was elected, using funds collected from public donors, including schoolchildren. After the Roosevelt presidency, the pool was also enjoyed by Harry Truman and later presidents. John F. Kennedy used it regularly to ease his chronic back problems. Lyndon Johnson liked to swim naked in the pool and once invited Reverend Billy Graham to join him.[58]

However, Richard Nixon wasn't a swimmer. Nixon liked bowling. Regarding the swimming pool, he decided on a cover-up. In this case, the cover-up involved the construction of a floor over the top of the pool and converting the space into the White House Briefing Room used for press conferences and media interviews. The pool was left intact, under the Briefing Room, and it is still used as a computer and telecommunication center.

Nixon's successor, Gerald Ford, was an avid swimmer. Before becoming president, he swam almost daily in a pool in his home in Alexandria. Ford announced plans for a new WH swimming pool in the first few days of his presidency. The location for the new pool was on the South Lawn of the White House grounds. When construction started and digging produced

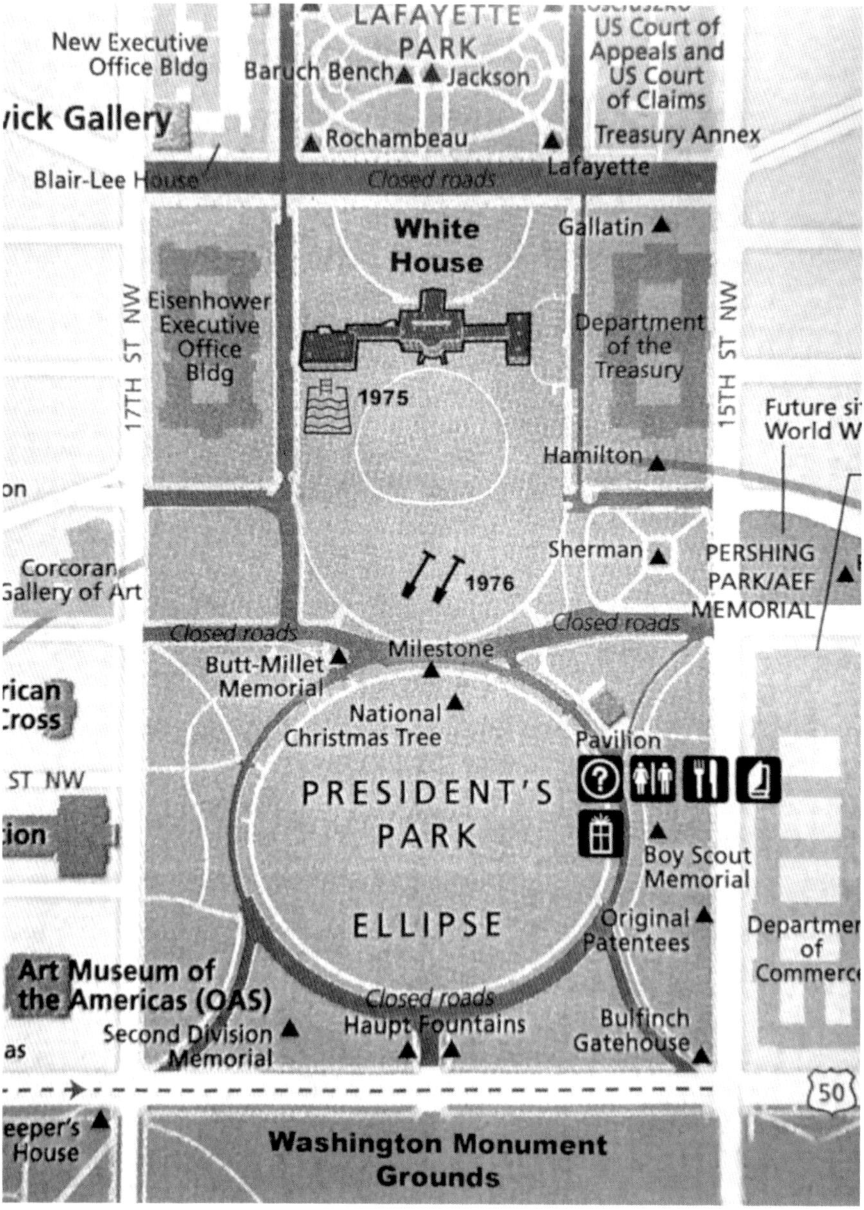

Above: Map of the White House grounds with artifact dig sites labeled. *Library of Congress, Geography and Map Division; modified by author.*

Opposite, top: President Gerald Ford overlooking construction of the White House swimming pool, 1975. *The Gerald R. Ford Presidential Library.*

Opposite, bottom: Artifacts from soil dug up for the White House swimming pool in 1975. *Drawing by Robert L. Humphrey, George Washington University.*

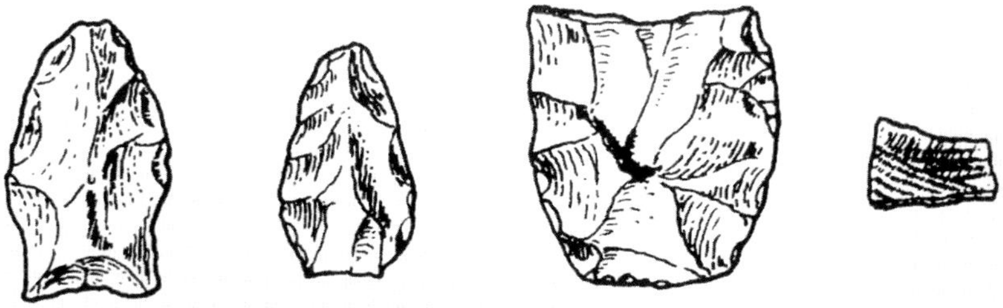

piles of soil form the south lawn, Robert Marshall, a curator for the National Park Service, spotted an arrowhead within one heap of the soil. That find led to a systematic screening of the excavated soil. It turned out that the fill dirt contained seventeen Native American artifacts, including two quartzite points and a pottery fragment.[59]

In the summer of 1976, Marshall conducted additional digs on the South Lawn of the White House grounds, working with college students. Those digs uncovered additional artifacts, including "a broken biface, a small projectile point, and a flake of quartz."[60]

Estimates of the time range for the White House artifacts do not indicate that any of them originated less than two thousand years ago.

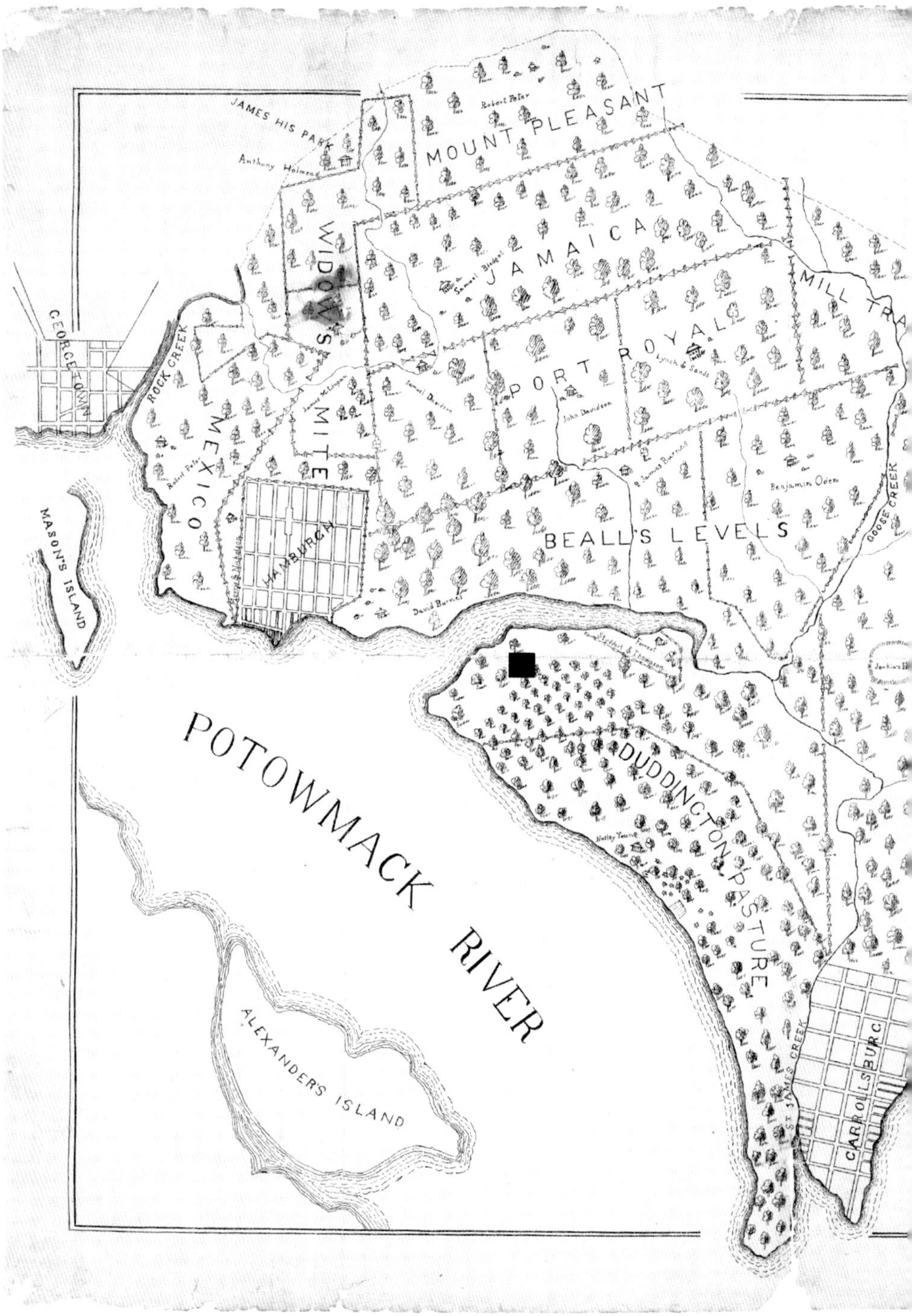
JAMES HIS PARK
Anthony Holmead
Robert Peter
MOUNT PLEASANT
WIDOWS MITE
JAMAICA
Samuel Blodget
PORT ROYAL
Lynch & Sands
John Davidson
Samuel Davidson
GEORGETOWN
ROCK CREEK
MEXICO
Robert Peter
HAMBURGH
BEALL'S LEVELS
Benjamin Oden
GOOSE CREEK
David Burnes
MASON'S ISLAND
POTOWMACK RIVER
DUDDINGTON PASTURE
Notley Young
ST. JAMES CREEK
CARROLLSBURG
ALEXANDER'S ISLAND

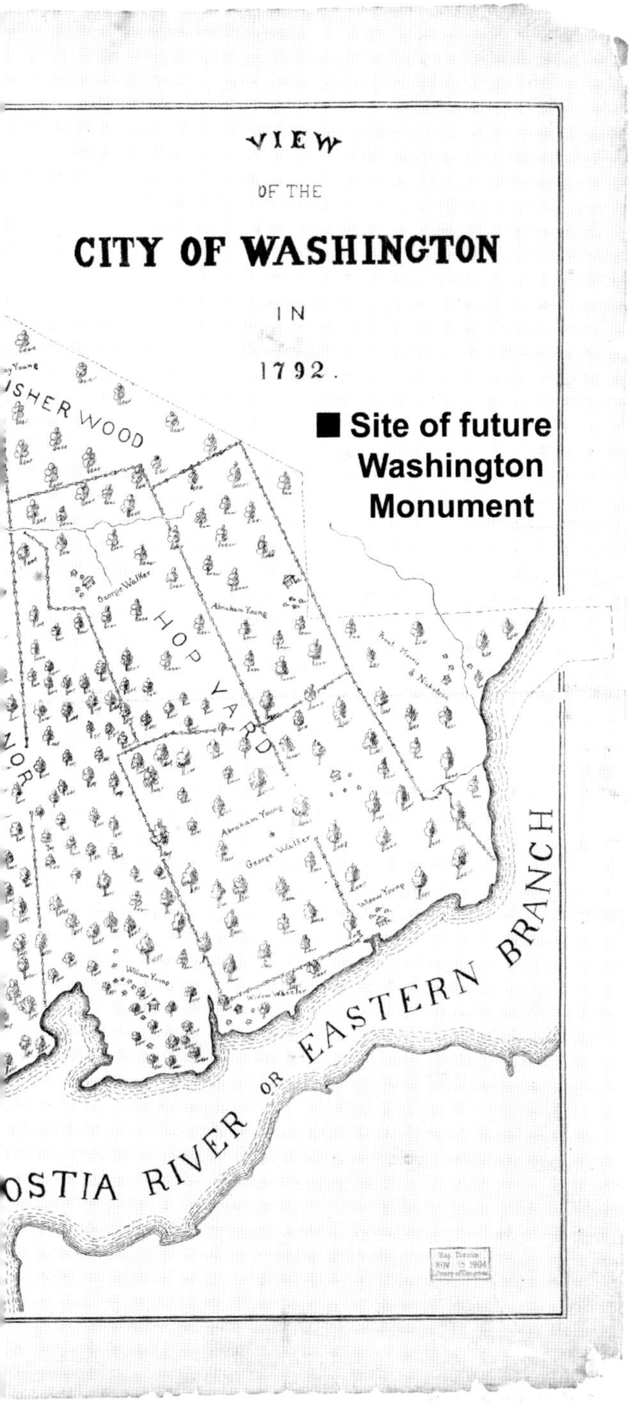

City of Washington in 1792 with future site of Washington Monument marked. *Library of Congress, Geography and Map Division, modified by author.*

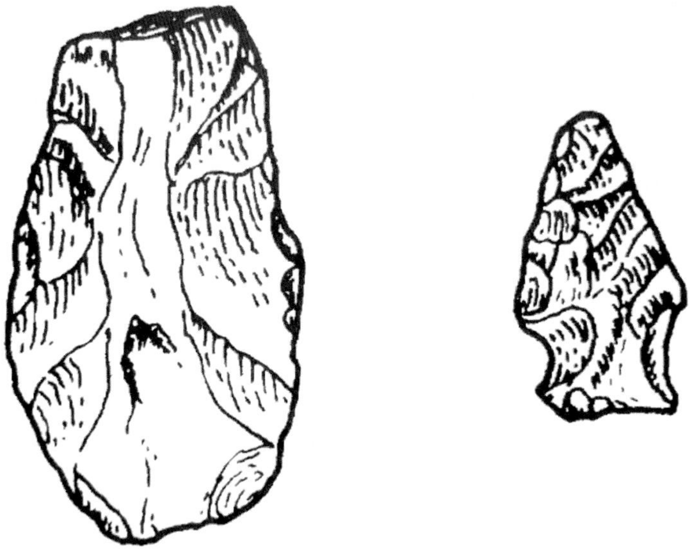

Artifacts from 1976 dig on south lawn of the White House. *Drawing by Robert L. Humphrey, George Washington University.*

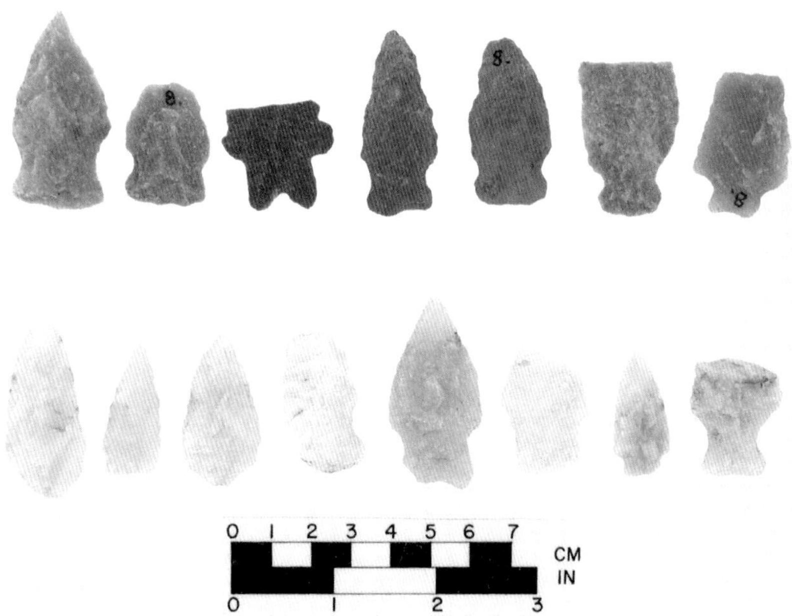

Native artifacts from the Washington Monument grounds. *J. Krakker, National Museum of Natural History.*

Therefore, these Native American artifacts were made by the ancestors of the Anacostans.

Native artifacts have also been collected from the nearby grounds of the Washington Monument. The monument grounds were once located on the Potomac shoreline. During the 1880s, over 140 artifacts were collected from the site, consisting of about 50 projectile points and a few ceramic potsherds.

These collections of artifacts on the White House grounds and nearby document a Native presence on an important site in modern Washington. Yet a scan of news reports from the late 1970s, when the most recent artifacts were found, doesn't uncover any stories that mentioned them. The reported details on the WH artifacts are all included in a short addendum to a George Washington University (GWU) article, "Ancient Washington,"[61] which was first published in January 1977. In the acknowledgements section of that article, the authors specifically express their appreciation to Robert Marshall for his contribution to the work.

It appears that Marshall contacted the archaeologists at GWU with his findings of the WH artifacts, which they included in their 1977 article. In 1986, Robert Engelman wrote a story for the *Washington Post Magazine*, "Washington Before Washington," that told many of the stories of Native Americans in the District.[62] One of his major sources in the article was Robert L. Humphrey, an author of the "Ancient Washington" article. Engelman included the story of the artifacts found at the White House in his article that ran in the *Sunday Magazine* on July 13, 1986. Despite this prominent citation, there's no indication that the story of the White House artifacts received attention in other media reports until 2018.

Although the artifacts story may have been privately discussed in academic circles, it was over thirty-five years later that the White House artifacts were mentioned in a *Washington Post* article in 2018 that reported on the work of the DC Native History Project.[63] Since that time, the White House Historical Association did a detailed story in 2019 on the swimming pool finds,[64] and the WH site is now included in a phone application, A Guide to Indigenous DC.[65]

It's sadly amusing to note the optimism that was expressed at the end of Humphrey's 1977 "Ancient Washington" article: "The increased awareness of the importance of research in this area promises that the capital's prehistory will not remain in the shadows."[66]

Unfortunately, more than thirty-five years later, we still have a long way to go before the important Native American artifacts found in the center of Washington are publicly displayed and explained to residents and visitors.

6

Foggy Bottom Burial Site and Artifacts Found in 1997

The Whitehurst Freeway is an elevated highway built in the 1940s to let traffic bypass Georgetown and connect the central downtown route, K Street, to the Key Bridge. It is only eight-tenths of a mile long. The skyway at K Street was conceived and planned by H.C. Whitehurst, who was director of the District Highway Department. Eventually, the K Street Skyway was named for him.[67]

The freeway was built before there was much regulation of historic preservation. The home of Francis Scott Key, the author of the poem that became "The Star-Spangled Banner," was originally located at what became the western terminus of the freeway. It was torn down to make way for the highway. After the Historic Preservation Act was made law in 1966, it became a prerequisite for all federal and state construction site planning to consider the possible disruption of historic and archaeological sites.[68]

In the 1990s, there was interest in building a new ramp for the Whitehurst Freeway. The mandated archaeological digs done before construction could be started uncovered three major sites with important Native American artifacts on the northwest edge of Foggy Bottom, the DC neighborhood adjoining the site.[69]

The three archaeological sites that were identified by this research were named the Peter House, Whitehurst West and Ramp 3. Each site contained a variety of Native American artifacts, and one contained the cremated remains of a once powerful woman.

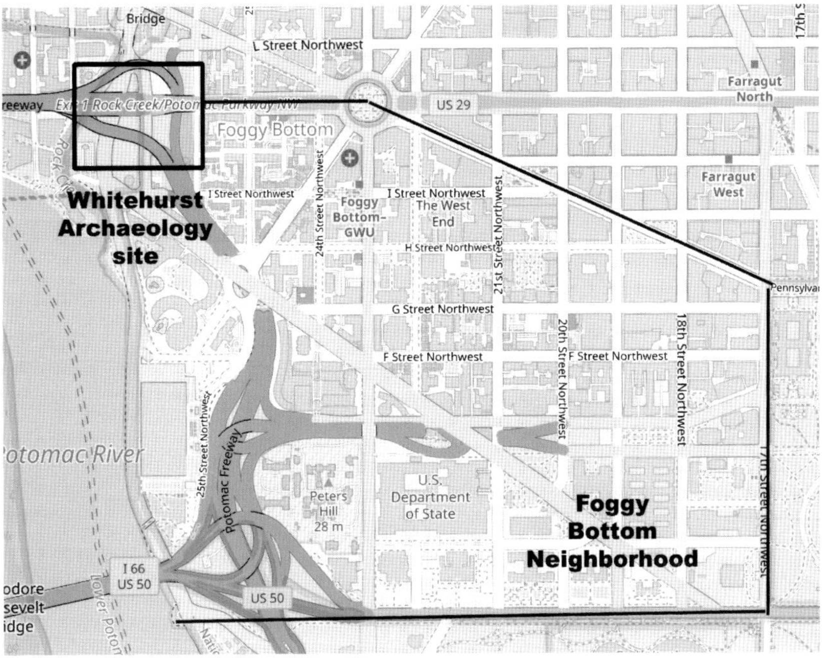

Map of Foggy Bottom neighborhood with Whitehurst Freeway archaeology site highlighted. *Open Street Maps, modified by author.*

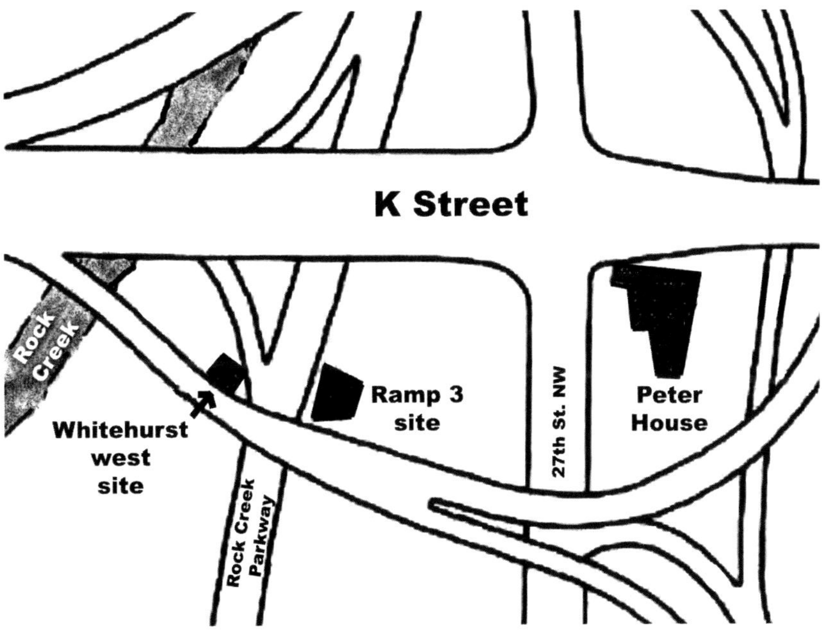

Map of Whitehurst Freeway ramp archaeological sites. *Drawn by author.*

The Peter House Site

This area once included eighteenth- and nineteenth-century houses that had been built over Native American artifact sites. The archaeological evidence about Native life showed that the sites that had once been used for fires—large amounts of fire-cracked rock were found—as well as tool making. Flaked rock was present in significant quantities, along with an extensive amount of pottery pieces. This suggested the area had been used for an extended time as a village site.

Based on the style of some arrowheads that were found, archaeologists estimated they may have been made more than five thousand years ago. However, some were of styles that suggest they were made during the five hundred years before colonists arrived in the 1600s. In two firepit sites that were identified, charcoal remains were found on pottery that were dated to around five hundred years before colonization.

The Whitehurst West Site

This site was closest to the edge of Rock Creek. Over time, the shoreline of the creek may have extended into this site, but the bulk of the finds at this site, which included ceramics and stone artifacts found with fire-cracked rock, charcoal and animal bones, indicated occupation within a few hundred years before the colonists arrived. The vegetation remains found at this site indicate that Native foods included pokeweed, hickory nuts, walnuts, raspberries and blackberries.

Ramp 3 Site

This site is below the Peter House site but on the east side of the Rock Creek Parkway. Two layers of artifacts were found here. The top layer was from the relatively recent past. Below that, however, was an older pit that had been capped with large stones. Around these stones, the archaeologists found burned earth and partially burned charred wood. Below that, in a shallow pit, a rich assortment of artifacts was found. They included a large slate pendant and a smaller schist pendant, fourteen great white shark teeth, a large triangular black chert knife blade, a stone phallus, burned human and large bird bones, eighty-three fragments of burned antler (later found

Ramp 3/Whitehurst Freeway burial artifacts. *National Park Service.*

to be an antler comb), six antler disks, one wooden bead and small pieces of preserved textile made from plant fibers.

The remains and artifacts at this site indicated that it contained the cremated remains and grave goods of a woman of high status. She may have been between thirty and forty years old when she died. Upon death, the body was cremated elsewhere. This pit was the final resting place of her remains. The cremated remains were placed in the pit with artifacts, including the pendants, phallus and an antler comb. Then a ceremonial fire was lighted and extinguished as the pit was filled.

What was striking to the archaeologists who studied these artifacts was that they were not typical of Native American burials in the mid-Atlantic region but had more in common with those found in areas ranging from Ontario, Canada, to Upstate New York, although similar sites have also been found in Virginia.[70] A speculative interpretation of this burial and the others found elsewhere indicated the woman who died was likely a prominent member of a tribal family who traded in high-value goods. The items buried with the woman were exotic and easy to carry, suggesting they were used in trading. The location of her burial also suggested that

Whitehurst archaeological sites 2022, unmarked. *Photo by author.*

her tribe may been powerful enough to have held control over a valuable river site involved in the annual fish runs, which still occur in Rock Creek. This burial site may be related to a large Algonquin trade route that once extended from Canada down to the Chesapeake, which would have been active at the time of the burial, about 1,200 years ago.

In a 2016 video presentation by Stephen Potter, retired regional archaeologist for the National Capital Region of the National Park Service, which is available online, Potter described this site, saying: "Ramp 3 is The (with a capital T) most significant prehistoric discovery in the city of Washington." Despite its significance, the site is still unmarked and uncelebrated.

ABSENCE OF OTHER ARTIFACTS FROM FOGGY BOTTOM

Considering the rich assortment of artifacts found in this northwest corner of the Foggy Bottom neighborhood and the location of the area, which also borders of the grounds of the White House, where other artifacts have been found, it is notable that no other sites in Foggy Bottom have been identified. Checking with a few sources in Foggy Bottom, including bloggers and a museum archivist, a common theme emerges to explain why additional sites have not been identified.

Heurich Brewery in Foggy Bottom. *Courtesy of Heurich House Museum.*

Foggy Bottom has a history of intense industrial activity. That history includes being the site of the former Washington Gas plant, where coal was converted to gas (24–26th and G Streets, NW). The offensive air pollutants that are given off in that process may have been the source of the term *foggy* in the area's name.[71] Foggy Bottom was also the location of the Heurich Brewery, now the site of the Kennedy Center for the Performing Arts. The area was populated by workers involved in those plants and building the future Capital City.

As we can see from the findings at the Peter House site, building over Native American remains did happen. In general, the early development of Foggy Bottom just didn't support the preservation of much older history. As is discussed in chapter 12, the ongoing development of the Palisades neighborhood in northwest DC presents a current conflict between development and the erasure of Washington's Native American history.

7

Henry Fleete

The Young Man Who Lived with the Anacostans for Five Years in the 1620s

The story of Henry Fleete is unique in American colonial history and an important part of the story of Washington's Native American people.

Fleete was a young English settler and the son of William Fleete, a member of the London Virginia Company, which sponsored the Jamestown colony. The twenty-two-year-old Henry Fleete arrived in Jamestown in early 1623 and was recruited into a trading party that sought corn from the local Natives.

The leader of the trading party was Captain Henry Spelman, who had come to Jamestown in 1609 as a fourteen-year-old. In that year, negotiations between Captain John Smith, then governor of Jamestown, and Chief Powhatan had Spelman and two other young men traded to be the chief's servants in return for permission to let Jamestown to stay on Powhatan's land. As Spelman later wrote: "Unknowne to me he sold me to him for a towne."[72]

Spelman used his time among the Natives to become fluent in the Algonquin language. Following his time with Powhatan, Spelman also lived with another Native tribe, the Patawomecks,[73] which is the tribe whose name led to the English word Potomac.

The Jamestown trading party of 1623 that was led by Spelman included Fleete and twenty-two other men. Because they had heard that the Anacostans had good supplies of corn, they sailed up the Potomac to the chief's village in hope of securing some.

Powhatan, American Indian chief. *Encyclopedia Britannica.*

It was March 1623 when the trading party arrived at the Anacostan chief's village. Spelman, Fleete and seventeen other men went to meet with the chief, and five men stayed on their boat.

The men on board the boat heard gunshots as fighting broke out. Natives trying to board the boat were fought off, and the trading party members who remained on the boat then fled back to Jamestown. Some versions of this story include a report that Spelman's severed head was seen on the shore by the sailors as they sailed away. Fleete was presumed to be among the dead. However, he was the only crewman who went ashore to survive.[74]

How Fleete survived and what happened to him after he was captured, including the five years he lived with the Anacostans, are not known. Fleete did leave a journal, which was written in 1631, and can be read at the Library of Congress.[75] In it, his only mention of the time with the Natives comes up indirectly when he comments on his skills in their language: "Considering that in my infancy and prime time of youth…I was for many years together compelled to live amongst these people, whose prisoner I was, and by that means am a better proficient in that Indian language than any one."

One suggestion about what happened after Fleete was captured by the Anacostans was that he was sold as a slave.[76] Using captured prisoners as servants was a practice among the Algonquins and seems to be a reasonable assumption.

There is an indirect clue that Fleete was taken as a servant by a powerful person in the tribe—perhaps a woman who had lost her husband and needed a helper. Fleete was captured in March 1623. In November 1623, to take revenge for the death of Henry Spelman and his crew earlier in the year, the governor of Virginia, Sir Francis Wyatt, allied himself with the Patawomecks tribe and attacked the Anacostans, burning their fields and killing several Anacostan warriors.[77] After that attack and the loss of many warriors in the tribe, the survival of the colonist living with the Anacostans would have required the patronage of a powerful sponsor.

After five years with the Anacostans, Fleete returned to Jamestown in June 1627. Some reports say he was "ransomed," but there are no clear references to when the people of Jamestown became aware that Fleete was alive and living with the Natives or on the terms of a ransom. It is likely that the Natives who brought Fleete back to Jamestown were given various items as a reward for helping return a fellow colonist. This might have seemed like a ransom to some. As additional speculation about Fleete's fate with the Anacostans, it is possible that his elderly sponsor had died, and since there wasn't much interest in keeping Fleete longer, the tribal leaders sent him back to Jamestown.

In 1989, Betsy Fleet, a descendant of Henry Fleete (the family now spells the name without the silent *-e*) wrote a book on her ancestor.[78] Unfortunately, the book is not well documented and contains a lot of speculation. However, in her book, she states that Fleete was freed by the Natives "in gratitude for his help in checking 'the great sickness.'"[79]

The introduction of European diseases had devastating effects on the Native Americans. Much like the lethality of the COVID-19 virus in our recent past, the Natives suffered terribly since they did not have previous exposure to common European diseases such as smallpox, measles or flu. Charles Mann, in his 2005 book, *1491*, describes what archaeological finds tell of Native American life before the arrival of European colonists, suggesting that disease was one of the major factors that reduced Native populations by nearly 90 percent after the colonists arrived.[80]

Details about disease among the Anacostans are not documented. In general, the Anacostans were not a tribe closely watched by the English settlers. Betsy Fleet's comment suggests that a "great sickness" occurred while Fleete lived with the Anacostans. Ironically, it is possible that Fleete was a major source of the agents that caused the sickness.

After his return to Jamestown, Fleete sailed back to England and organized a plan to come back to the Chesapeake with ships and goods to become a trader in the region. There is an intriguing comment made in a 1627 letter to Joseph Mede, a biblical scholar at Cambridge University, regarding Fleete's return to Jamestown. The letter, which was sent from London by someone who had apparently heard Fleete talk about his time with the Anacostans, says Fleete had lived with the Natives so long that initially "he hath left his own language."[81] Thus, after five years of life with the Anacostans, Fleete seems to have arrived in Jamestown not able to recall much English!

When Fleete again returned to the colonies, his skills in the Algonquin language and Native customs gave him a major advantage over other merchants interested in the furs and tobacco that the Natives could offer, and he became a successful trader in the Chesapeake region. His success and that of other colonial traders indirectly struck another blow to the survival of the Anacostan tribe by disrupting their previous dominance in trade.

Fleete died in 1661. By the 1660s, life for the Anacostans had become so tenuous that the Anacostan chief and his entourage moved north from the tribe's established trading location, which was on the Potomac, near the mouth of the Anacostia River. Details on the Anacostan village sites are discussed in chapter 9.

8

The U.S. National Arboretum Native Village Site

In his writings, Proudfit identified two Native village sites close to the west bank of the Anacostia River. The Garfield Park/Carroll Estate (chapter 2) was one. The second of these sites was located at what is now the U.S. National Arboretum.

As discussed in chapter 2, Proudfit identified the village site on the Carroll Estate as an outgrowth of his work overseeing the construction of Garfield Park. Proudfit seems to have identified this second village site because much of his archaeological research around DC was done in the Benning Road area on the east side of the Anacostia. Late in his life, Proudfit donated his catalogue of Native artifacts to the Smithsonian Institution, and it has been digitalized, so every page can now be viewed online.[82] Inspecting his catalogue of artifacts shows that at least 80 percent are labeled "Benning." The National Arboretum site is only about a mile from Benning, so over time Proudfit probably walked the nearby west bank of the Anacostia, across the river from Benning, and found the second site.

Proudfit described the Arboretum site's location as "on the west bank of the Anacostia and southeast of the Reform School."[83] Maps from the late 1800s show the U.S. Reform School Farm running along Eastern Avenue down to the Anacostia. The U.S. Reform School was started in the 1870s as part of a national movement to incarcerate young people with criminal convictions separately from adults. In the history of the institution, which was later renamed the National Training School for Boys, one of its most notorious residents was Charles Manson, who was sent there in 1951 when

Hickey Hill and the Anacostia River. *Photo by author.*

he was convicted at age sixteen for driving a stolen car across state lines, a federal crime.[84] The institution was closed in 1968 and redeveloped as the current Fort Lincoln neighborhood.

The village site marked by Proudfit on his map seems to correspond to what is labeled on other maps as Hickey Hill. One of the earliest developers of the farms that were situated near the Anacostia was Colonel William Hickey (1798–1866). He and his descendants owned various tracts of land in the area, and Hickey Hill Road can be found on old maps. It is still the main road that leads to the site in the National Arboretum.

The congressional authorization to create the National Arboretum was passed in March 1927. The site was considered suitable because there were no permanent buildings on the land, and the soils and climate were favorable for a large variety of plantings. Land was purchased by the government in various parcels in 1928, 1934 and through the 1940s. Initially, development of the Arboretum was slow, but notable progress was made by the Civilian Conservation Corps (CCC) in the 1930s.[85] As was common at the time, the CCC was segregated into white and Black camps. The crew that worked in the Arboretum was a Black group; during their work, they found Native American artifacts on the grounds.[86]

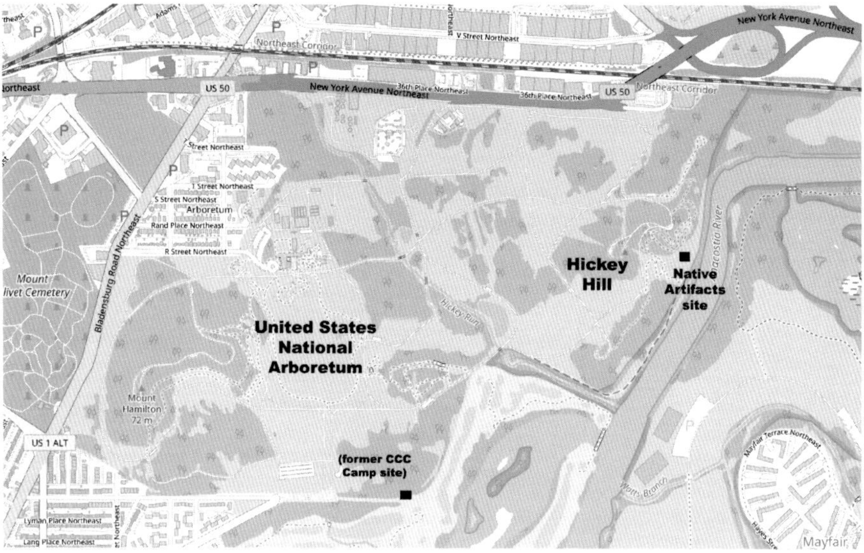

National Arboretum map with sites labelled. *Open Street Maps, modified by author.*

Although news reports of the 1930s describe the CCC camp and some of their work, a public citation of the Native artifacts that were found by the CCC workers was first included in a 1973 document used to secure a listing for the Arboretum in the National Register of Historic Places.[87]

A search for where the artifacts from the National Arboretum have been stored, unfortunately, led only to dead ends. Perhaps when the Arboretum staff gets to work on telling the artifact story to visitors, they will have luck in locating them.

9

The Anacostan Chief's Village and Native Burial Grounds—Now the Anacostia-Bolling Military Base

Chapter 1 describes how Captain John Smith and his mapmakers traveled up the Potomac and made contact with the Anacostans. To determine the location that they identified for the Anacostan chief's village involves a bit more detailed discussion of their map.

The Smith map, which was first published in 1612, includes a cartographic image that is called a compass rose. This symbol was used to indicate the orientation of the map in terms of north, south, east and west. The overall shape is based on four petals of a rose pointing to the cardinal directions. During the 1500s, the fleur-de-lis symbol was used to represent north, which points to the right side of the map. Using this clue to the orientation of the Smith map, when it's overlaid on a modern map of the juncture of the Potomac and the Anacostia Rivers, the location of the icon representing the "king's house" corresponds to the land south of the mouth of the Anacostia on the east bank of the Potomac.

When not under attack from another tribe, the Anacostans would live in small groups of wigwams in a pattern that has been termed "dispersed settlements."[88] The layout of a chief's village would be more elaborate and most likely correspond to the John White drawing of the village of Secotan.

Like most Native living sites, a chief's village would have gardens. But the complex life of a chief would also require sites for ceremonies and group fires. Since the Anacostans were noted to be traders, the chief's village would be likely to include a site where visitors met with the chief or his helpers to conduct trade.

Left: Map compass rose from Smith 1612 map. *Library of Congress, Geography and Map Division.*

Below: Map symbols from Smith 1612 map. *Library of Congress, Geography and Map Division.*

When John White saw Secotan, which was used for the basis of his drawing, he may have been attracted by all the many aspects and features of the village but unaware that it was the village of a local chief.

In Captain John Smith's writings, he estimated the chief's village to include 80 able men.[89] In writings by others in the early 1600s, the Anacostans were estimated to be a tribe with about 340 members.[90] Both of these estimates could have been inaccurate and would not be the only time that population estimates have been wrong.

Secotan Native village, De Bry engraving. *Library of Congress, Prints and Photographs Division.*

Smith wrote that members of the tribe greeted him warmly, in contrast to the tribes in the lower Potomac that were influenced by Powhatan, who had not approved of Smith's exploratory voyage.[91]

Smith also gave flowery descriptions of the richness of the land and water in the area near the junction of the Potomac and Anacostia Rivers. In one case, the density of fish around his boat led his crew to try catching fish with a frying pan:

> *That aboundance of fish, lying so thicke with their heads above the water, as for want of nets (our barge driving amongst them) we attempted to catch them with a frying pan: but we found it a bad instrument to catch fish with: neither better fish, more plenty, nor more variety for smal fish, had any of us ever seene in any place so swimming in the water, but they are not to be caught with frying pans.*

Because the Potomac falls prevented Smith from sailing farther upriver, he sailed back to Jamestown and finished his first voyage exploring the Chesapeake on July 21, 1608.

The land around the chief's village had been surveyed by colonial settlers in the early 1660s. In 1663, Thomas Dent (1630–1676) was given a land grant, by Cecil Calvert, 2nd Baron Baltimore, that included the tribal lands. Lord Baltimore spent his life in England, overseeing his charter of land from the king of England. The land in Baltimore's charter was a rental from the king of England with an annual fee of one-fifth of all gold and silver found and the delivery of two Native American arrows to the royal castle at Windsor every Easter.[92]

As discussed in earlier chapters, the Anacostan tribe had gone into hard times during the sixty years since the colonists first arrived. Their numbers were reduced by the new diseases brought from Europe. Battles with colonists and other tribes had also killed off warriors and interfered with their farming.

A major treaty was signed between the colonists and the Piscataways in 1666.[93] The Anacostans participated in the negotiations for that treaty. The land that was set aside for the Piscataways was the site of their king's village at Accokeek, Moyaone (pronounced "Moy-own"). That land is now Piscataway Park, run by the National Park Service, and the burial site of an important modern Piscataway chief, Turkey Tayac.

After the 1666 treaty was signed, the Anacostan chief must have realized he had no assurances regarding the traditional land of his tribe. Two years later, the chief and his entourage of Anacostans moved off their traditional land and settled for ten years on the island upstream in the Potomac that we now know as Roosevelt Island. A map published in 1673, when the Natives were living there, shows the island named "Anacostien Island."[94] Later derivations of the island name were "Analosten" and "Analostan."

After the Anacostan chief moved, Thomas Dent established a plantation on the large tract of land along the Potomac that included the former site of the chief's village. Dent named the tract in honor of his home village in England. The Yorkshire village is Guisborough, but the name eventually came to be spelled "Giesboro."

Tobacco was the crop that the colonists grew and exported profitably throughout the seventeenth and eighteenth centuries. John Rolfe began growing tobacco in Jamestown in 1612. By 1630, over one and a half million pounds of tobacco were being exported from Jamestown every year.[95] Growing tobacco required a lot of farmland. Tobacco rapidly drains the soil of its nutrients, so after about three growing seasons, land had to lie fallow for three years before the soil could be used again.

Dent lived until 1676, and his family stayed on the land until 1715, when it was sold to Colonel Thomas Addison. About 150 years later, in 1863, George Washington Young bought the plantation. Young rented some of the Giesboro land to the Union army to create the Giesboro Cavalry Depot, which during the Civil War years held as many as thirty thousand horses in reserve for use in local battles.[96] This rental agreement began a pattern that led to a series of deals with the federal government for that land, which eventually led to the establishment of a permanent military base, now called the Joint Base Anacostia-Bolling (JBAB).

Although Proudfit may have been commenting on his finds in nearby areas, his 1889 description of the extent of the remains to be found in these areas probably also applied to the Giesboro tract: "These fields have been under cultivation for many years, and are regularly visited by local collectors, yet they are to-day, in places, fairly strewn with the wreck of the old village life."[97]

With the advent of airplane flight during the early 1900s and their use in World War I, the U.S. Navy began using the northern portion of the Anacostia for seaplanes in late 1917 and established the Naval Air Station Anacostia in 1918. Colonel Raynal Bolling was a staunch advocate of what was then a new idea—the use of airplanes in warfare. Bolling was killed in France in March 1918, and the airfield in Anacostia was named for him.[98]

In the following decades, the Bolling Base was expanded, but it was in 1936, during work to extend the runways on the air base, that a remarkable find was made: two Native burial sites were found near Giesboro Point.

In 1936, the growing Bolling Air Base gained access to farmland on the southern end of the base, allowing the lengthening of its runways. On September 11, a bulldozer operator uncovered bones when he moved some soil.[99] Work in that area was halted, and the DC coroner was called to inspect the bones. No record of burials during recent decades could be found for that site, and the coroner concluded that the bones were those of American Indians. The following day, Dr. Thomas Stewart, an archaeologist from the U.S. National Museum of Natural History, part of the Smithsonian Institution, arrived at the site to inspect what was found. The descriptions of this discovery were covered by the *Washington Post*[100] and the *Evening Star* newspapers[101] and eventually described in a 1937 journal article by the investigators from the National Museum.[102]

When Stewart arrived at the site, he at first found only a few bones and a skull that had been uncovered the previous day. The bones collected earlier had been put in barrels, and Stewart suspected some of the skulls may have been taken by workers.

This pit of bones was about 150 yards from the Potomac waterline. While Stewart and the other Smithsonian staff were examining that site, workers uncovered a second pit of bones about fifty yards east of the first pit. Stewart and his colleagues were able to excavate the second pit by hand during the next two days.

The soil covering the second pit was only a few inches thick, and bones located near the top had apparently been broken by past plowings of the field. This pit contained bones spread in an irregular space about fifteen feet in diameter and sat only six to eighteen inches below the surface.

Historical records indicate that Native American burials in the mid-Atlantic region included several practices. Captain John Smith described individual burials that included bodies wrapped in skins or mats, buried with their jewels in single pits. A painting of John White shows a structure called a "charnel house," where groups of bodies were placed to dry before the bones were collected into groups and buried in a common site. This type of burial site is termed an ossuary, and it seems to be the type found and examined by Stewart and his colleagues on the Bolling grounds.

As reported in the 1937 journal article, the pits contained bundles of long bones—arm and leg bones, from several skeletons, found together—and skulls, or parts of crushed skulls. The bones came from men, women and children—the size of jawbones can be used to identify children. The ages of the children were estimated to range between one and six years. The investigators determined that the two burial pits contained about 130

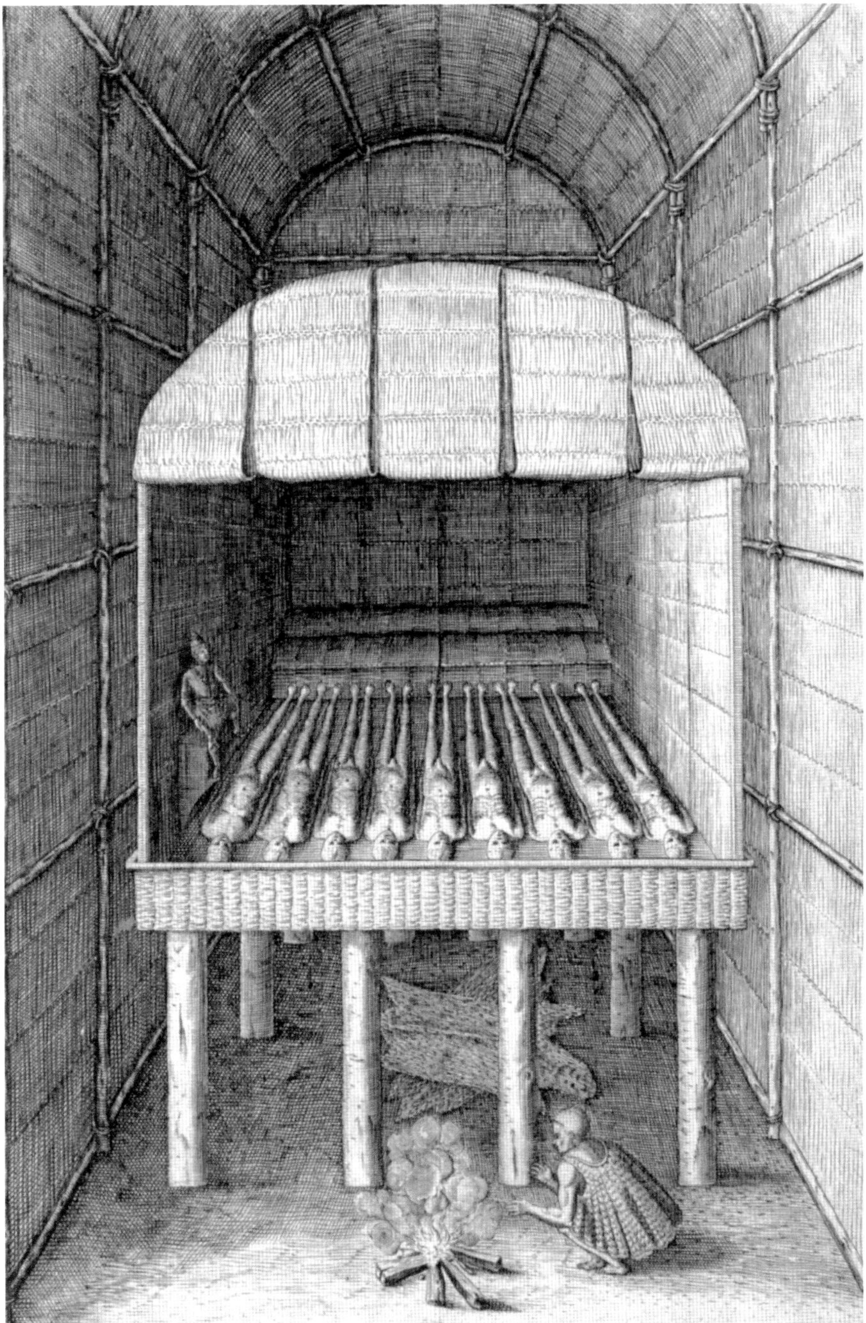

Charnel house with bodies, De Bry engraving. *Prints and Photographs Division, Library of Congress.*

skeletons, 16 of which were children. Measurements of various bone and skull features indicated that the Natives buried at the sites were typical of those found in other eastern American Indians. Examination of the teeth found in the two pits indicated that the incidence of dental cavities was rather common among the buried Native Americans.

Unlike other burial sites in the Chesapeake region, there were very few beads and ornaments found with the Bolling burials, although one skull did contain fourteen small shell beads. No metal, glass or other materials that would indicate a European presence during the burials was found.

In discussing the overall significance of finding these burials near Giesboro Point in their journal article, the authors emphasized the demonstration of the Native American presence in that area and the likelihood that the burials had been located near the Anacostan chief's village, north of the burial grounds.

The recognition of this complex Native history on the grounds of JBAB remains an ongoing discussion. Beginning in the summer of 2019, the DC Native History Project and two Piscataway tribes began asking for some acknowledgement of this history from the base command. Although some progress seemed to be forthcoming, in the fall of 2021, the command of the base shifted from the Department of the Navy to that of the Air Force. After

Joint Base Anacostia-Bolling gate, 2022. *U.S. Navy photo by Lieutenant Commander Jim Remington.*

resubmitting a summary of the base's Native history to the new command, it was encouraging to learn in April 2022 (personal email) that two tribal liaison officers had been designated by the Air Force to work on the many other standing issues. A small victory also occurred in April 2022 when the online summary of the base history was amended to open with mention that the Anacostan tribe once lived on the land.[103] Meetings between the JBAB command and the Piscataway leaders are ongoing about how the history of the base could be more extensively acknowledged to the public.

A second major and complex issue involved in the history of JBAB will be the reburial of the bones from the burial pits, which is called "repatriation." It seems likely that the bones are included among stores of more than eighteen thousand others held by the Smithsonian Institution.[104]

10

The Native Canoe Found near the Navy Yard and the Native Fishing Site Found next to Washington, DC's New Soccer Stadium

Some details of the Native American history of DC have been recorded solely in newspaper reports and never given detailed study by archaeologists. One of these news items described the remains of a Native canoe that was found in 1871 during construction of a railroad tunnel not far from Garfield Park.

In the early 1870s, the Baltimore and Potomac Railroad dug a tunnel in southeast Washington to connect the Anacostia Railroad Bridge to the old train station that sat where the National Gallery of Art building is now located. The tunnel ran under Virginia Avenue, near the Navy Yard.

A brief report of local news from the *Washington Evening Star* on August 15, 1871, said workers had excavated an Indian canoe at the depth of about forty feet.[105] The first question that comes to mind about this news item is how did a canoe get forty feet underground? The answer to this question involves both the original geography of the area and the complex history of landfills in Washington that started in the late 1700s.

Examination of old maps shows that there was once a stream that fed into a shallow bay near where the tunnel was being dug. St. John's Bay, which no longer exists, extended up to what became Virginia Avenue. Reference to the geography of the site reveals that, in terms of sea level, forty feet below the surface is where the water level would have been when the Native Americans lived on this land.

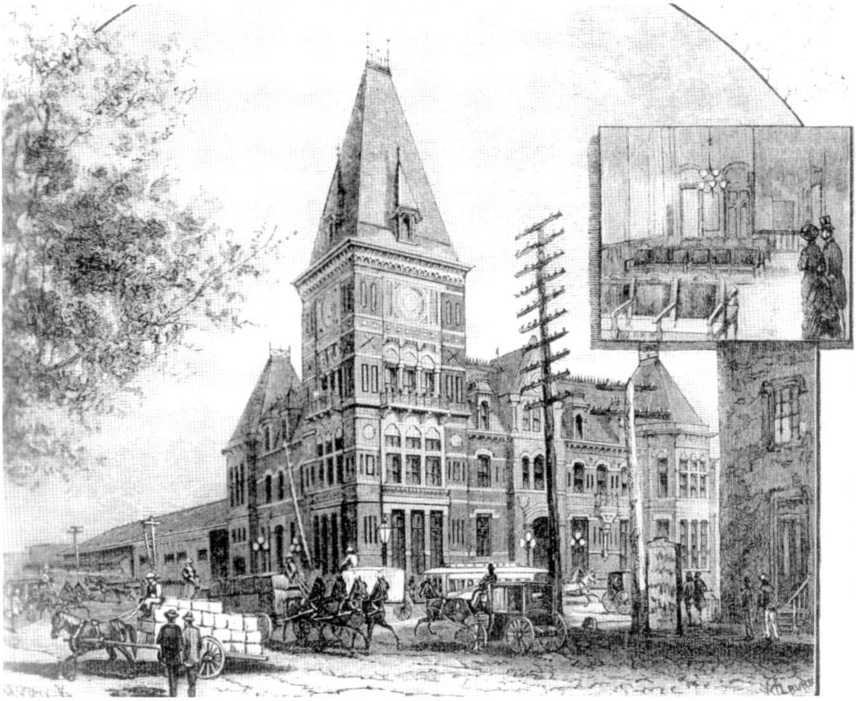

Baltimore and Potomac Railroad Station, Sixth and B Street NW, Washington, DC, as it appeared in the 1880s. *Prints and Photographs Division, Library of Congress.*

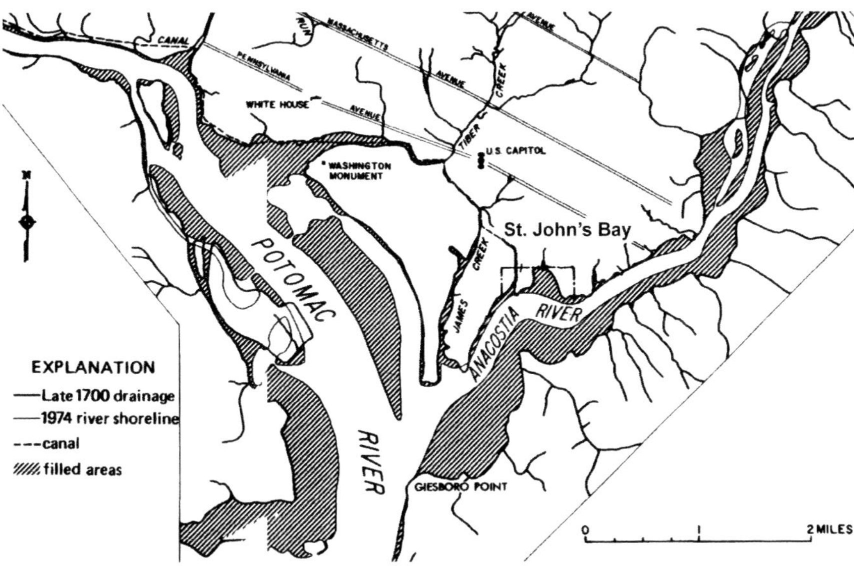

Map of Washington, DC, showing James Creek and St John's Bay fill. *Library of Congress, Geography and Map Division, modified by author.*

So, the canoe was right where it was left in the past. The fill for the bay and the land that ran through southeast where the tunnel was being dug could have come from several nearby sites, including the grounds of the Capitol. The land for the Capitol had been flattened during construction, but old topographic maps indicate that the original hill of Capitol Hill included a twenty-foot peak, which was located on the land where the Library of Congress Jefferson Building now sits.[106] That peak, cleared by enslaved laborers as part of the construction of the Capitol, had to be moved somewhere. St. John's Bay and the streambed not far from the Capitol would have been a convenient destination for the excavated fill. Unfortunately, detailed records to document the source of the fill materials for the stream and bay are unavailable.

There is a second article describing the odd fate of the Indian canoe, which never received close examination at the time. The second article explains that the workmen found the canoe and broke it up to save as relics before it could be inspected by the engineer overseeing the work site.[107] But this brief description of the fate of the canoe may provide a clue about what type of canoe was found.

Native Americans building a dugout canoe, DeBry engraving. *Prints and Photographs Division, Library of Congress.*

Native Americans collecting wild rice in a birchbark canoe. *Prints and Photographs Division, Library of Congress.*

Natives in the Chesapeake region constructed two basic types of canoes. The biggest and strongest canoes were dugouts, made from the largest species of local trees, tulip poplar. Dugouts were made from tree trunks that were hollowed out using controlled fires. The burnt wood was removed using a chipping tool called an adze. Some dugouts were reportedly fifty feet long and could hold forty warriors. A second type of canoe built by the local Natives was smaller and lighter, consisting of a frame made from a water-resistant wood, such as cedar, and the bark from elm or birch trees stretched over the frame. These canoes were so water resistant that, under some circumstances, the Natives would put rocks in their canoes to sink them underwater to keep them hidden.

Although the workers involved in the tunnel building would probably have tools adequate to cut up a dugout canoe, the apparent speed at which the found canoe was dismantled by the workers suggests it was probably a bark canoe.

Most details about the canoe are lost, but the news reports provide another demonstration of the Native presence in the southeast portion of Washington, within a mile of where the Capitol stands.

The Native Fishing Site Found next to Washington DC's New Soccer Stadium

Local interest in the southwest quadrant of Washington uncovered an 1866 article from the *Washington Evening Star* describing what seemed to be a Native fishing village that was located along the creek that once ran through Buzzard Point in southwest DC.[108]

As shown in the map on page 85 that includes St. John's Bay, the creek that split the land on Buzzard Point was James Creek, a continuation of Goose Creek that at the time ran at the base of what became Capitol Hill. These creeks were fed by the numerous springs that once sat at the top of Capitol Hill and eventually were channeled into sewer lines as the area was developed. In the 1860s, James Creek was built up into a canal in the hopes of improving the use of the waterway for boats and businesses. The news article reported that while the creek was being dredged, a number of

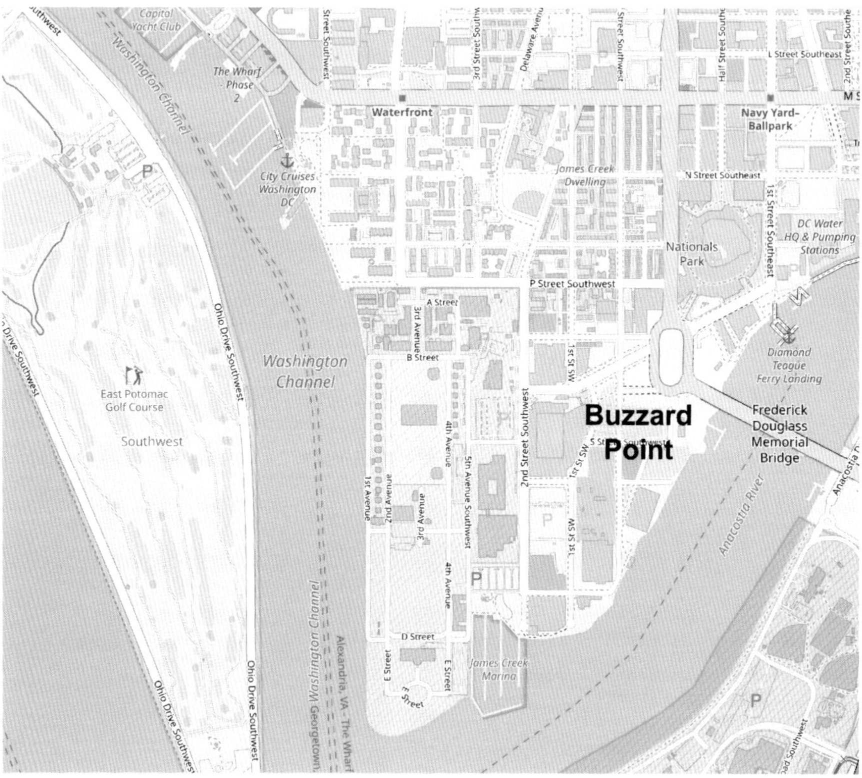

Buzzard Point Map. *Open Street Maps, modified by author.*

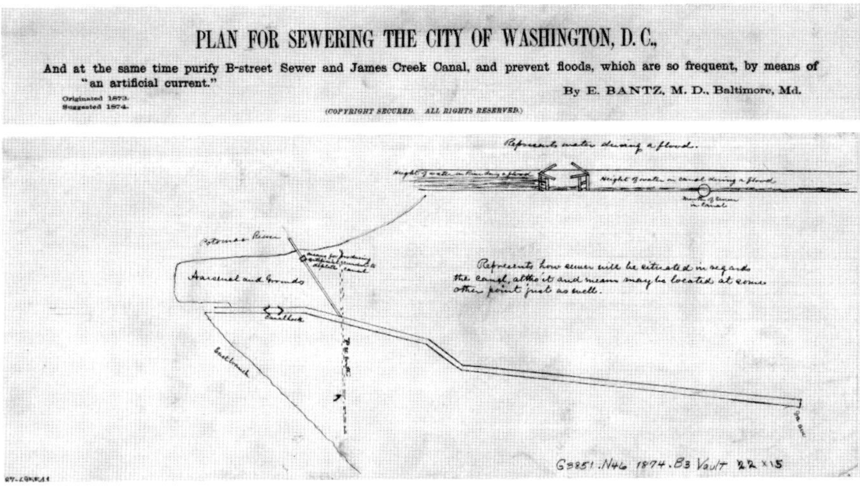

The James Creek Canal from the 1874 Plan for Sewering the City of Washington, D.C., by E. Bantz. *Library of Congress, Geography and Map Division, modified by author.*

Native American artifacts were found in one spot along the shoreline. This spot was enclosed within about a thirty-foot area and included axes, spears, arrowheads and pestles. The pestles would have been used to grind seeds and corn.

Consistent with the thoughts of Proudfit about sites where more than just hunting items are found, the article concluded that the site was once used by the Anacostans as a possible fishing village along the river. Unfortunately, this is another site where the fate of the found artifacts is unknown.

11

Anacostia Metro and Barney Circle Artifacts, the Native Pot Found in 2009

Anacostia Metro Artifacts

In the early 1980s, archaeologists excavated land along Howard Road, SE, before construction began on the site of the Anacostia Metro Station. The excavation revealed traces of a Native American camp on the Stickfoot Branch, a small stream that once ran through the future Metro site and emptied into the Anacostia. The stream had been rerouted into sewer lines in the late 1800s and largely covered over when the Suitland Parkway was constructed in the 1940s.[109]

Estimates of the ages of the artifacts ranged back several thousand years, indicating that the area was a commonly used site for Native life near the river, not far from where the Anacostan chief had located his village. The artifacts are currently held by the Anacostia Community Museum (ACC), which is part of the Smithsonian Institution. Although not regularly on display at the museum, some of the artifacts can be viewed online.[110] The artifacts that were found in the 1981 digs included hide scrapers and stones that would be used for working the local quartz and quartzite found in the area to make arrowheads and pointed tools. The archaeologists identified two places where Natives had dug out cobblestones and shaped them into blade forms. Another nearby area was found where the blade forms were made into finished tools.

Construction in this area before the passage of the 1960 laws regarding historic preservation would have overlooked and probably destroyed traces

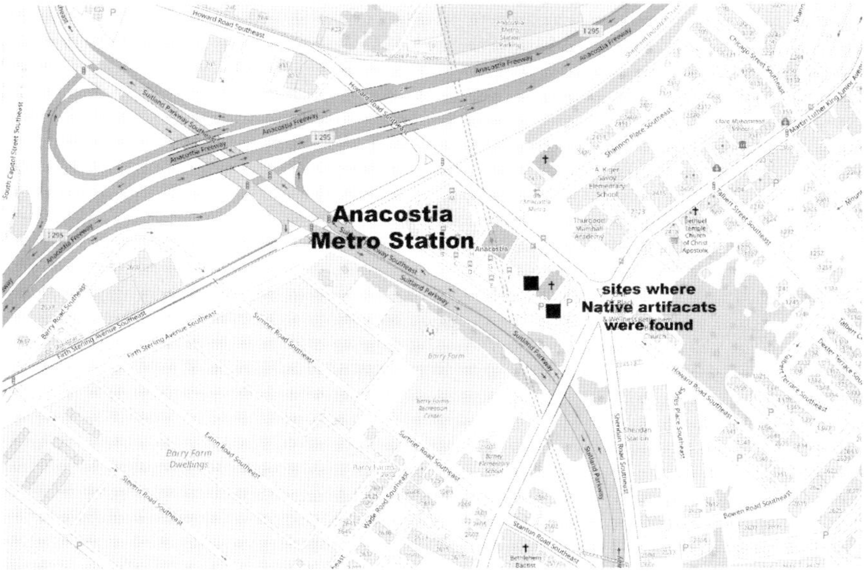

Map of the Anacostia Metro Station and Howard Road with artifact dig sites labeled. *Library of Congress, Geography and Map Division, modified by author.*

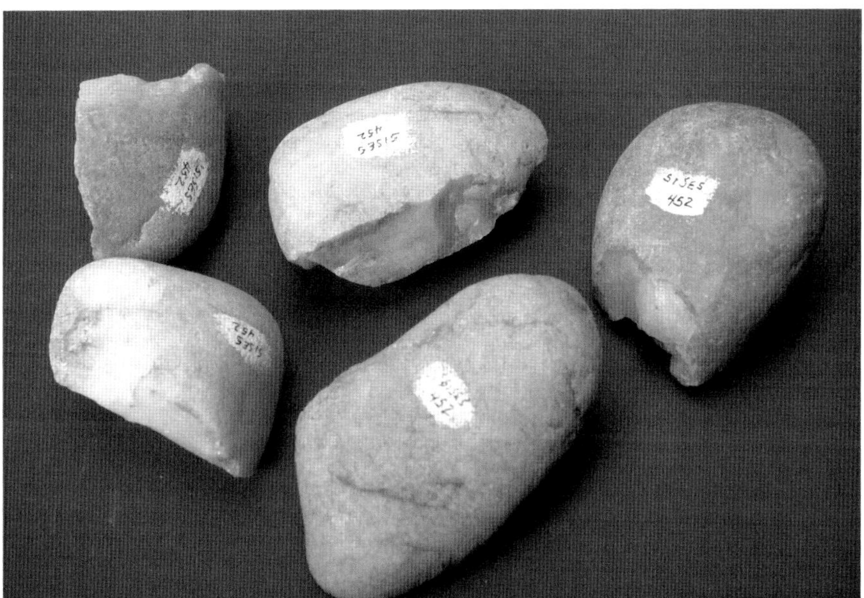

Anacostia Metro Native artifacts—cobble stones. *Courtesy of the Anacostia Community Museum.*

Anacostia Metro/Howard Road lithics. *Courtesy of the Anacostia Community Museum, photo by author.*

of the Native life that once existed there. Although the archaeological record was established for the site, there are no public markers of its historic significance at the Anacostia Metro Station or elsewhere in Anacostia. Access to images of a few of the finds are available online, but they are not displayed to the public at the ACC.

BARNEY CIRCLE ARTIFACTS

Barney Circle is a neighborhood in southeast DC that sits near the Anacostia River, north of Pennsylvania Avenue. The archaeological digs done along the Anacostia River on the edge of Barney Circle were prompted by a 1975 plan to build a new freeway that would have run along the west bank of the river. The digs were carried out as part of an environmental impact review that is required of all federally funded development projects.[111] Based on earlier finds, detailed archaeological digs were done in 1994, which provided a basis for the public pressure against the project, leading to the rejection of the project by the DC City Council in 1996.[112]

In 1994, four major dig sites were studied: two on the east bank of the Anacostia and two on the west bank that adjoins the Barney Circle

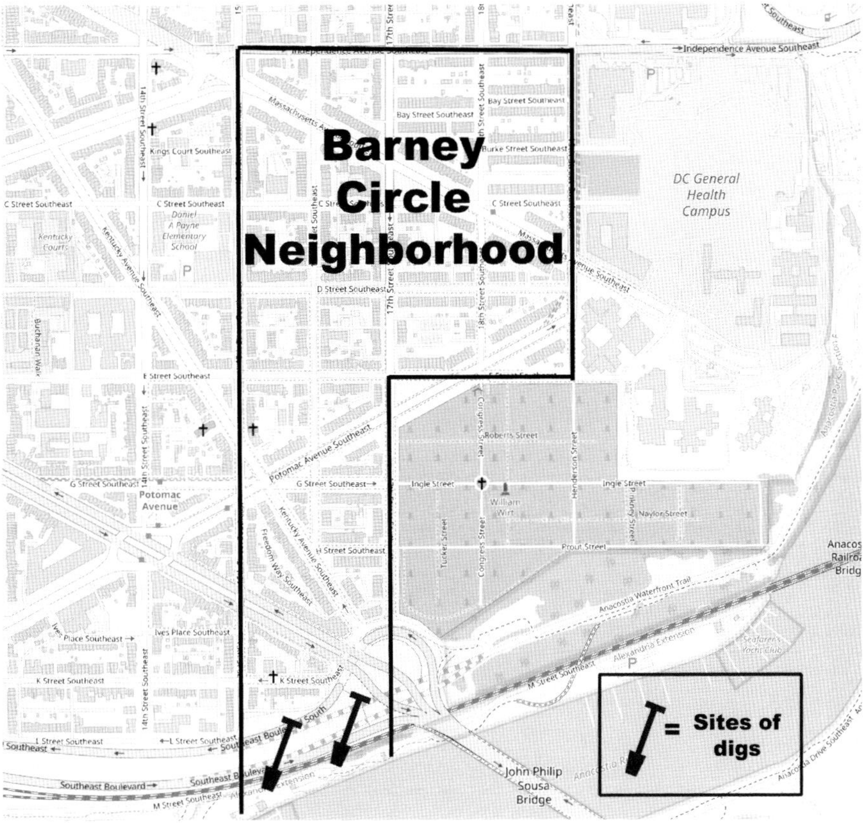

Map of Barney Circle with artifact dig sites labeled. *Open Street Maps, modified by author.*

neighborhood, next to the Congressional Cemetery. At the two sites on the west bank of the river, archaeologists were puzzled at first because they found artifacts such as spear points and pottery shards that were dated to older periods than what was later found at lower levels in the dig.[113] Further analysis of historic maps revealed that the top layers of soil comprised fill from buildings that had been demolished above the sites. The fill dirt was used to raise the marshy ground surface.

Analysis of the stone points and pottery found at the sites indicated that they had probably been used by small groups of Natives about 1,500 to 3,000 years ago. The pottery shards and clusters of heated rock from the sites suggested that they built fires to cook foods, including the wild rice and fish harvested from the river.

The earlier preliminary archaeological work and the detailed work done in 1994 were important elements in motivating public opposition to the

Barney Circle pottery artifacts. *Courtesy of the DC Historic Preservation Office, photo by author.*

Barney Circle bifaces. *Courtesy of the DC Historic Preservation Office.*

freeway construction. The finds made it apparent that the proposed road construction would have effectively destroyed Native sites that had important historic significance.

As noted in the 2013 report on the Barney Circle sites,[114] the archaeological sites were not completely excavated, and large parts were left untouched. This was due not only to the time and expense required to fully excavate the sites but also because archaeologists often leave a portion of a site intact for future research that may have the advantage of enhanced investigative techniques.

THE NATIVE POT FOUND IN 2009

As noted briefly in chapter 9, the land that comprises the Joint Base Anacostia-Bolling (JBAB) was under the jurisdiction of the U.S. Naval Command until 2021, when it was transferred to U.S. Air Force. In 2009, the Naval Command was interested in building a connector road on the north end of the Bellevue Housing Complex, which is on the southern edge of the military base. As part of the planning, an archaeological investigation was undertaken of the site to be compliant with the Historic Preservation Act of 1966.[115] That investigation uncovered several Native artifacts from an area that seems to have once been a village site. The details of the finds were reported at a 2011 conference by Gregory Katz, a member of the Louis Berger Group that was contracted to do the work.[116]

The early history of this area was described in chapter 9 regarding the Anacostan chief's village and the Native burial ground. The Bellevue Housing site was about half a mile from the sites where the ossuaries were found in the 1930s. The military housing development of the Bellevue site began in 1941, when World War II defense workers poured into Washington. The development included 601 single-family housing units constructed on cinder block foundations with no basements. In the 1990s, these houses were razed, and the area was left open as a recreation field.

Previous archaeological digs had been conducted in the area, and they uncovered pottery fragments, some in the backyards of houses that remained occupied. A conclusion drawn from the earlier digs, using clues found in the recovered artifacts and pottery fragments, was that the area encompassed a village site dating back about one thousand years. It was largely because of these earlier finds that the site was left undeveloped.

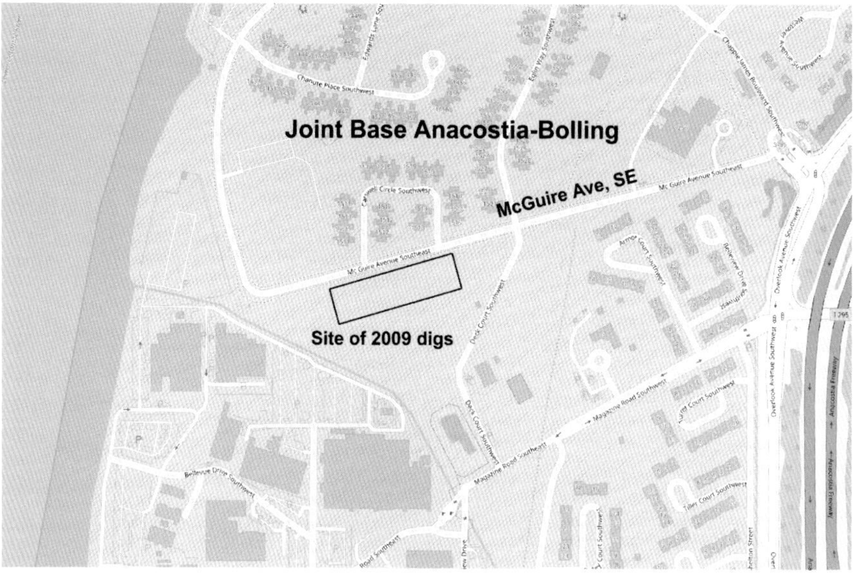

Joint Base Anacostia-Bolling 2009 dig sites that recovered a Native American pot. *Open Street Maps, modified by author.*

In the archaeological survey of 2009, test digs in an area of about an acre in size identified remains of a hearth, six filled holes where Native poles once stood (post molds) and fragments of a ceramic pot that was complete enough to be reassembled. The pot that was found was classified as "Accokeek" because this style of pot was first described in archaeology studies that were done in Accokeek, Maryland, at the site that was once the village of the major chief of the Piscataway Indians called Moyaone (pronounced Moy-own). The Moyaone site is about twenty miles south of the JBAB base, also on the eastern shore of the Potomac.

This style of pot, which has been found throughout the Chesapeake, was made with a coil of clay that was compressed to form the shape of the pot. The pot's surface was then smoothed and imprinted by pressing a paddle wrapped in cord onto the surface before it was dried. The pattern that has been associated with Accokeek pottery was an oblique cord-marking, slanting to the right from the vessel rim.[117]

More than 150 pot fragments that were collected at the Bellevue site were reassembled by the staff of the James-Patterson Park Museum in St. Leonard, Maryland, where the pot is now stored.[118]

Although 40 percent of one side of the pot was missing, various techniques allowed for the reconstruction of the bulk of the pot. It was cone shaped,

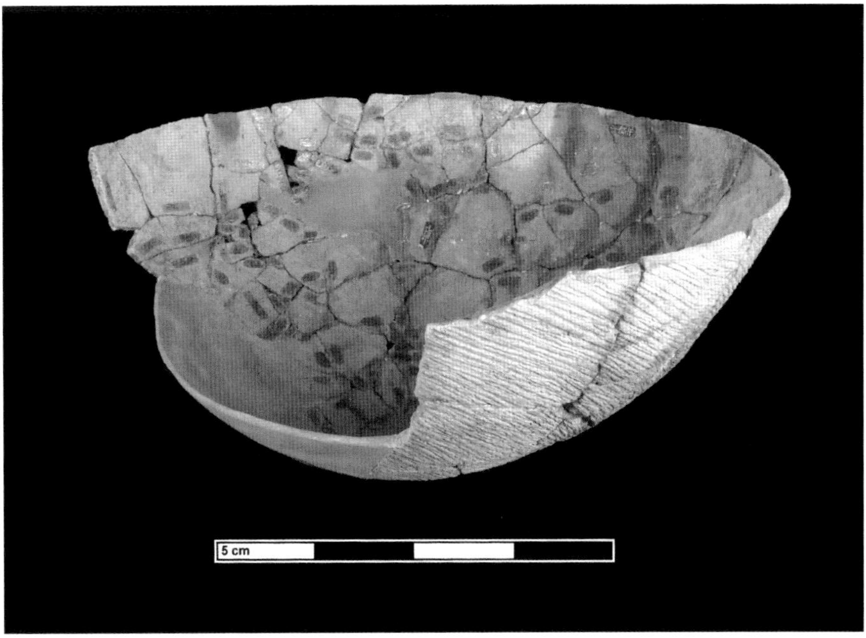

Reconstructed Native American pot found in 2009. *Courtesy of the Naval District Washington, Joint Base Anacostia-Bolling. Photo by Caitlin Shaffer.*

Native Americans cooking in conical pot. De Bry engraving. *Prints and Photographs Division, Library of Congress.*

with a diameter of sixteen inches and a depth of eight inches. Cone-shaped pots were depicted in the drawings of John White. The shape allowed the pot to be placed into a fire pit and propped up during cooking.

The ironic survival of extensive parts of this Native artifact was captured in the title of the 2009 article written about the Bellevue site: "Bellevue's Telltale Heart (51SW7): Accokeek under the Floorboards."[119] The title references the classic Edgar Allan Poe story about a killer who is haunted by sounds he hears that seem to come from his victim, whom he had hidden under the floor of his house. Since the previous Bellevue military housing was built on cinderblocks, this Native pot had survived undisturbed by the construction while under the floorboards of one house.

The story of the Native pot and other archaeological finds at the Bellevue site, combined with the documented earlier record of the burials on the grounds of Bolling, show the extent of the Native history there. However, as was also noted earlier, though available to military leadership for decades, this rich Native history has not been presented in any form by the base's leadership. American Indians serve in the armed forces at a higher rate than any other demographic.[120] This site's history has been hidden not only from the general public but also from the many Native Americans who have proudly served at Bolling.

12

Sites Near the Potomac River

Native Storage Pits at Fletcher's Cove, the Maddox Branch Sites and the Palisades Neighborhood

Having focused on the Native history surrounding the land once occupied by the chief of the Anacostans, as well as older Native sites in central Washington, DC, it is time to detail the rich stories of finds that have been made along the Potomac River in the northwest quadrant of the city, below Little Falls.

The small waterfalls in the Potomac, known as Little Falls, mark the ridge that exists between the two geologic areas that cross through Washington. The north is part of the Appalachian Piedmont (literally "foot of the mountain"), and the south of the city is continuous with the Mid-Atlantic Coastal Plain.

In the city, this ridge marks what was the edge of the oldest part of Washington. The original name of the road that ran at the base of the hill it formed was Boundary Street. It is now named U Street and Florida Avenue.

The neighboring Iroquois tribe that lived north and west of the Piscataway referred to the Anacostans and other Picataways as "the people who lived below the falls." The Algonquin word for this phrase, Kanawa, is believed to be the origin of the name Conoy for the Anacostans and the Piscataway tribes.[121]

Little Falls marks the "fall line" for the Potomac, where boats cannot travel any farther upriver without portaging. This barrier to river travel generated a variety of responses from the Native Americans, and many aspects of their efforts can be seen in sites along this section of the Potomac. They include a group of unique storage pits that were dug by

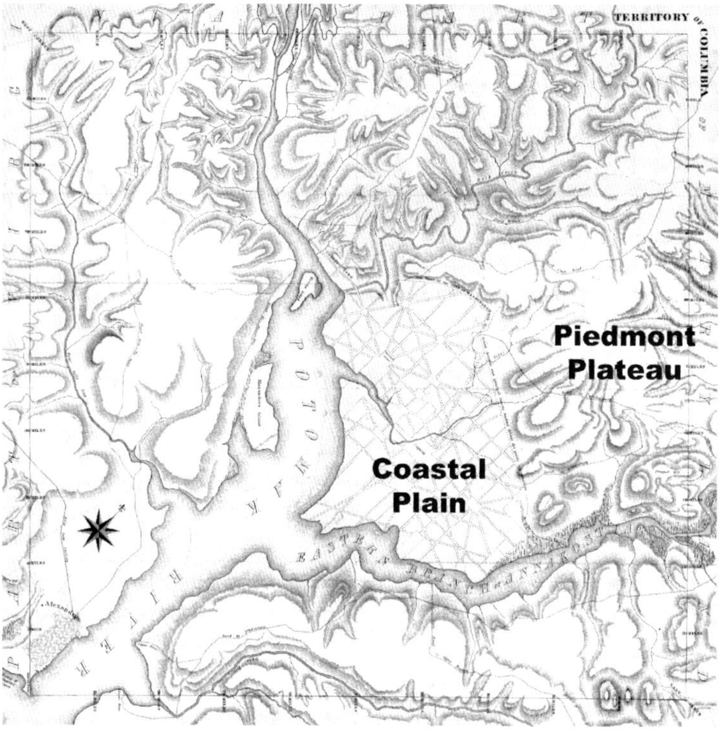

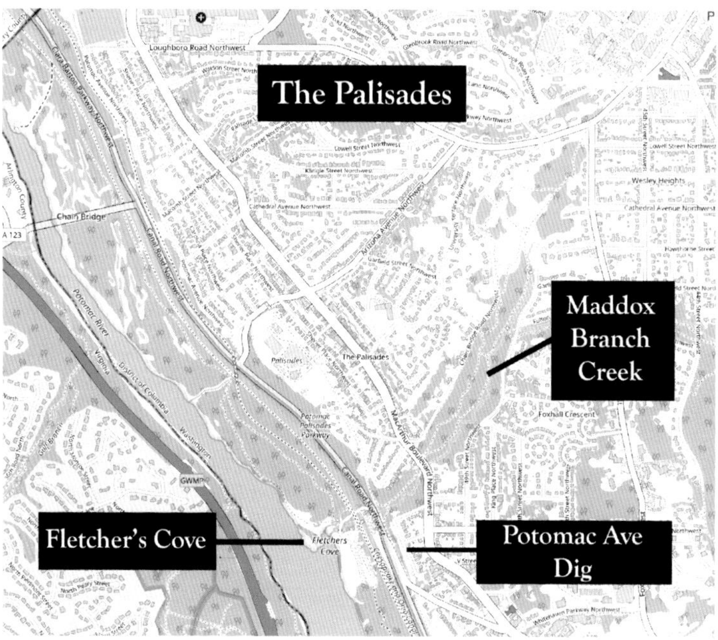

Top: A 1793 map of "Territory of Columbia," by Andrew Ellicott. Relief map showing piedmont plateau and coastal plain portions of the city. *Library of Congress, Geography and Map Division, modified by author.*

Bottom: The Palisades neighborhood with key archaeological sites labeled. *Open Street Maps, modified by author.*

Natives next to the river, and a rich variety of Native artifacts that have been found along a creek that drains into the river just below Little Falls, the Maddox Branch. The numerous artifacts still being found in what is now the Palisades neighborhood of Washington, DC, which sits above the Falls, on the east side of the Potomac, also demonstrate the extensive history of Native life in this area.

THE STORAGE PITS FOUND AT FLETCHER'S COVE

Located just below Little Falls, Fletcher's Boathouse rents rowboats, canoes, kayaks, bikes and paddleboards for use in the Potomac and along the C&O Canal Towpath. It sits on a small cove that was formed by the runoff from the Maddox Branch Creek that empties into the Potomac.

In 1997, the NPS wanted to make various changes to the area around Fletcher's Boathouse to improve visitor access. Before those improvements could be made, archaeological work had to be completed in order to comply with Section 106 of the National Historic Preservation Act.[122] One aspect of the new construction was a planned handicapped access ramp for the C&O Canal trail and the boathouse. Archaeological digs in that area uncovered a wealth of Native American history that is unique for the entire Atlantic coast of the United States.

Details on what was found there were reported in the *Washington Post*[123] and in an extensive summary from the archaeologists contracted to study the site.[124] A comment from one of the site investigators called the findings "fascinating…to say the least!"[125]

The study began with clearing an area to expose the ground's surface from when the C&O Canal was constructed in the early 1820s. Below that level, the investigators found about four feet of deposits built up by the Potomac River that dated back over eight thousand years. Buried along the river at a depth estimated to correspond to about two thousand years ago, the archaeologists found eleven pits, some seven feet in diameter and five feet deep. During the archaeological research, each of the pits was cleared of fill and the contents examined. The contents of the pits included debris from the building of newer pits and refuse that the Natives accumulated during their occupation of the site.

The researchers noted that none of the pits overlapped, and each was located to avoid another pit. In some cases, only a few inches separated one pit from another. The distribution of pits indicated the Natives could see

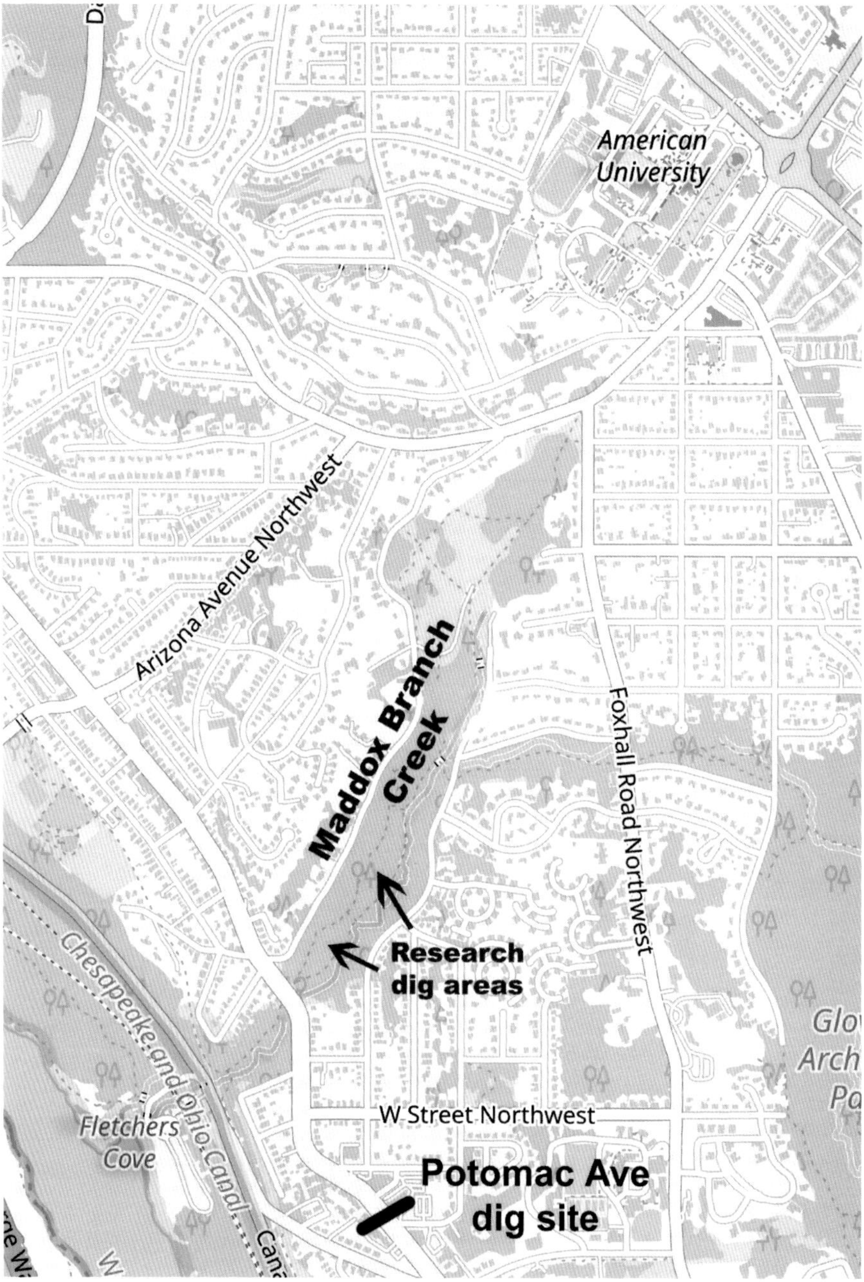

Map of Maddox Branch Creek, showing Fletcher's Cove and site of Potomac Avenue archaeological dig. *Open Street Maps, modified by author.*

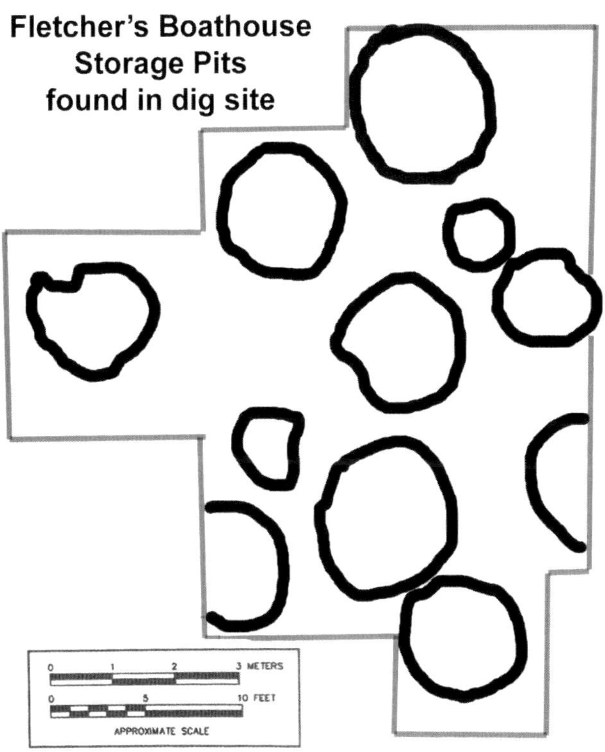

Above: Archaeological dig at Fletcher's Boathouse, 1997. *Courtesy of Richard Teehan/Friends of Fletcher's Cove.org.*

Left: Fletcher's Boathouse storage pit diagram. *Redrawn by author from original report, Barse, 2002.*

abandoned pits, and their proximity made it convenient to use an older pit to dispose of soil dug to create a new pit.

The investigators concluded that the pits were dug by a single group of Natives over time. This could have been an extended family or group of families that returned to the site each year, perhaps in the fall to collect and store nuts and other foods. Estimates of the age of the pits indicated they were dug in the period before farming became common among local Native people, so the Natives who built the pits lived as hunters and foragers. In the colder months, they had to hunt and use their stored foods, like dried fish, meat and nuts. In spring, annual fish runs of shad and herring would provide new sources of food. During the warmer months, Natives could move freely, living off the land foraging for other foods.

All the pits were found to contain an assortment of stone points and fragments of various types of Native ceramics. Archaeologists use the style of ceramic pieces and the shape of stone points to identify the periods when they were made. An underlying assumption for this identification system is that all craftspeople in each period made ceramics and stone points in the fixed style. Although this is a useful assumption that provides a framework for estimating the period when archaeological finds originated, the rigidity that it applies to craft work is questionable. A craft person could have decided that an older ceramic bowl or arrowhead had a style that was worth reproducing. Also, work in stone involves knapping to create a shape. An inadvertent break might produce a shape that varied from the norm for a period but still proved useful.

Putting these considerations aside, the archaeological estimate from the items found in the storage pits suggested they were all built about the same time, nearly two thousand years ago. Although Native storage pits have been found in various other locations along the Atlantic coast, most of those date to about one thousand years ago, after the time that Natives Americans began farming. No sites containing a cluster of large pits like those found at Fletcher's Cove have been found elsewhere in the eastern United States.[126] Other sites that have been found with similar sized pits contained carbonized corn, indicating they were used to store grains. However, these pits did not contain signs of cultivated foods but were found to contain some nut fragments, mostly hickory. This indicated the pits might have been used by Natives during seasonal occupations in the late fall and early spring for storing harvested nuts for later consumption.

Other pit sites that have been identified in the mid-Atlantic were associated with "post molds," the shapes left in the ground where there was once a wooden support pole. Typically, these posts suggest an area was covered for protection. No signs of post molds were found around the Fletcher's pits.

The archaeologists speculated that Native village sites might have existed near the pits, but the canal construction and other development would have eliminated those remains. As is explained in the next section, on the Maddox Branch Creek, extensive evidence of Native American life near this area has been documented.

The analysis of the ceramic fragments in the various Fletcher's pits indicated that they had a remarkable similarity in their styles. This was another indicator to the investigators that the pit builders were a relatively close group who returned to the site and repeatedly built new pits in the distant past while living there.

Another line of speculation as to why the pits were built focused on the possible use of these pits by Natives who were traveling upriver. The pits could have been used for storing provisions before portaging canoes around the falls. This leads to a discussion of the rich Native artifacts that were found along the creek that fed into the Potomac at Fletcher's Cove.

SITES ALONG THE MADDOX BRANCH CREEK

A creek runs down the hill that begins at the southern end of what is now the campus of American University in northwest Washington and empties into the Potomac at Fletcher's Boathouse (See map of Maddox Branch Creek, on page 102). The boathouse is built on the small cove formed by that stream.

One of the first studies that focused public attention on the Native history of the area around the Maddox Branch came from an archaeological investigation conducted by American University in 1972.[127] The digs by these investigators were located near the Maddox Branch, just north of Reservoir Road, on a strip of undeveloped land west of Potomac Avenue. The presence of Native artifacts in the area was common knowledge to nearby residents and artifact collectors. While the American University archaeologists were doing their digs, one of the nearby residents, George Birch, shared with the investigators over thirty mounted arrowheads that he had collected from his yard and nearby public gardens.

The digs by the American University group uncovered a line of post molds and two small pit features, which they interpreted as a wall of a large structure. Using ceramic pieces found during the digs, the site was estimated to be from one thousand years ago. Their overall conclusion was that they

The George Birch collection of Native artifacts from the Palisades neighborhood. *Photo by Doug Dupin.*

had located what was a small Native fishing camp. The American University group noted that access to the river by way of the streambed through the steeper portions of the terrain was probably a common route used by Natives. This would also be the primary route used by Natives who portaged their boats around the falls in the Potomac.

A more extensive archaeological study was commissioned in 1997 by the National Park Service to investigate sites farther north on the Maddox Branch.[128] The investigators in this group repeatedly noted in their report that the sites they were able to search for artifacts were rare in the Washington, D.C area. The Maddox Branch site had not been disturbed by development since the time when Native Americans had occupied them. The steep and relatively narrow valley of the Maddox Branch was not suitable for farming. Nearly a mile south of the Battery Kemble Civil War installation, this lower portion of the valley had not been significantly disturbed by nineteenth-century construction for the defense of Washington from Confederate attack.

Typically, Native American campsites were on high ground above rivers or along the banks of rivers. Therefore, there was never a plan for archaeological digs in the narrow valley of the Maddox Branch. But in 2004, archaeologists exploring the valley inspected the root ball of a tree that had recently fallen across the stream. Root balls are a way for archaeologists to get an easy glimpse of exposed deeper soil. Sometimes root balls contain buried artifacts. In this case, the root ball they examined contained three spearpoints and a piece of decorated Native pottery. These clues led the archaeologists, sponsored by the National Park Service, to do detailed studies in the Maddox Branch valley and uncover an extraordinary record of previous Native life.[129]

In their detailed final report, the archaeologists state that the density of the artifacts they were able to collect was surprising. Working in two defined test sites, they found that some archaeological test digs contained 1,000 to 1,900 artifacts in each three-by-three-foot square. Another small test site recovered 24 projectile points and 182 sherds of pottery.

The Maddox Branch creek. *Photo by author.*

A root ball. *Photo by author.*

An overall analysis of the many ceramics and worked stone points that were collected indicated that the Maddox Branch valley had been used repeatedly from about 2500 BC until after AD 1000. It seems that this small, protected valley—in most cases only fifty to seventy-five feet wide—was used by Native Americans who were camping at the foot of Little Falls, possibly for winter shelter or to keep their presence hidden from enemies. As mentioned previously, this valley was also part of a portage route around the falls.

The common occurrence of ceramic from pots and bowls found in the digs suggested to these investigators, as they did for earlier archaeologists like S.V. Proudfit (chapter 2), that women were part of the villages, preparing food at the location. The ceramic styles suggested that Native Americans lived in the valley from about 1200 BC to 1600 AD.

Among the artifacts found in the Maddox Branch Valley was a pitted grinding stone that would have been used for processing nuts. Other artifacts indicated that stone tools were made in the Native camps. These included an unfinished axe and discarded stone points, indicating weapon repair. Also found among the valley artifacts was a large, grooved axe, indicating heavy woodworking—tree felling or perhaps dugout canoe manufacture.

At most sites in the District of Columbia, the stone tools are made from two types of stone: quartzite and quartz. In contrast, the Maddox Branch sites included tools made from several different materials. Quartz and quartzite are common in the area, but the rhyolite (a volcanic stone related to granite) and chert (a stone similar to flint) found at Maddox Branch indicated that these stone items had been brought in from the west. Finding this assortment of stone among the artifacts suggested that the site was used by Natives traveling in bands from the west and south, as well as local Native Americans. This site, near the Potomac River, offered Native people a richness of foods, which ranged from birds and other game in the woodlands to the fish runs of shad and herring and resources such as nuts and fruits in and around the river valley.

Descriptions of Native life by John Smith and other early explorers suggest that the Algonquin Indians lived in villages only for part of the year, during the seasons of planting and harvesting corn. As mentioned previously, in the late summer and winter, small groups left the villages to hunt, fish and gather other foods. The camps in the Maddox Branch valley may have been used mainly by wandering bands in the autumn. This observation is supported by the large nut-grinding stone found among the artifacts. The shelter of the valley would also make it an attractive camping site during the cold and winds of the fall and winter.

Since the Maddox Branch valley was incorporated into public lands early in the development of Washington, DC, the authors of the 2008 report closed their commentary by remarking on the good fortune that protected the valley from being developed.[130] They compared the valley to the relatively undisturbed quarry sites that had been studied by W.H. Holmes and others (chapter 4) nearly a century earlier. They also noted that it was possible that small, repeatedly occupied Native base camps were not a unique phenomenon related to the Maddox Branch valley and that many similar sites could have once existed in the District of Columbia. However, traces of those sites were destroyed by urban development (see also chapter 6).

THE PALISADES

Sitting above Fletcher's Cove, on land located above the west side of the Maddox Branch Creek, is the northwest DC neighborhood called the Palisades. Not surprisingly, this area has also been a rich source of Native American artifacts.

The area covered by the Palisades runs from the edge of the Georgetown University campus (at Foxhall Road) to the DC-Maryland boundary (near the Dalecarlia Treatment Plant). Of course, these boundaries had no meaning for the Natives of the area, and there are important archaeological finds north of this neighborhood, along the Potomac and the C&O Canal recreation area.

One notable archaeological find north of Washington is the Hughes site, which included village remains and burials, such as the one shown here of two young men, probably brothers, who were buried together. The finds at this one site, first studied during the 1940s[131] and later extensively studied by a university group,[132] demonstrate the potential richness of the Native American history that awaits further discovery and recognition along the Potomac, north of Washington.

Proudfit showed several Native villages along the Palisades on his 1889 map and clearly stated how extensive the artifacts were in the Palisades:

> *The most important of these is the one stretching along the eastern shore of the Potomac from the lower reservoir to the Little Falls. This site lies on a table-land overlooking the river and at the base of another line of hills which rises from the eastern side of the plateau. The extent of this village is nearly equal to that of Nacotchtanke (Bennings), and it affords the same abundance of relics, which do not differ materially in character from those found at the latter place.*[133]

The area described by Proudfit became the Palisades neighborhood when it was developed for housing in the early 1900s. Earlier development in that area had included the Great Falls Electric Railway that carried passengers from Georgetown to Glen Echo Park. This followed a route that is now the street named Sherrier Place. There was also a bicycle raceway that was built in the 1890s by one of the major developers of the Palisades, Jacob Clark, that was closed in the early 1900s. It was then that the land in the area was divided into lots and sold for housing construction.

The archaeological study along Potomac Avenue described previously[134] involved research digs along the lower portion of the Palisades, closer to the Potomac River. As those investigators reported in 1972, one of the nearby residents, George Birch, shared his extensive collection of arrowheads that he had collected in that area (see "The George Birch collection…" image on page 106). The upper part of the Palisades is a larger area, which also has a history of local collectors finding artifacts on their property or at

Map of the Palisades, 2003, by Dan Dalrymple. *Courtesy of Dan Dalrymple.*

Burial found at Hughes site in 1940. *Courtesy of the J. Patterson Park and Museum Library.*

nearby sites. The street marker welcoming visitors to the Palisades includes Natives canoeing and shows the neighborhood takes its Native American history seriously.

For the last twenty years, the leading artifact collector and popularizer of the Native American history of the Palisades has been Doug Dupin. Dupin got started in 2003 when he decided to build a wine cellar next to his home in the northwest of the Palisades.[135] When he started digging, Dupin found that the first five feet of soil consisted of just clay fill. As he dug deeper, however, he found artifacts from various earlier periods, including Civil War materials as well as Native American pottery shards and a stone projectile point. During the next six months, Dupin expanded his dig to a fifteen-by-fifteen-foot seven-foot-deep pit, from which he sifted the bottom two feet of soil for artifacts.

The assorted artifacts collected in this dig, as well as others found in the yards of nearby Palisades neighbors, at construction sites and on parkland, were first assembled into a makeshift display at the Dupin home. In March 2006, he incorporated the display as the Palisades Museum of Prehistory.

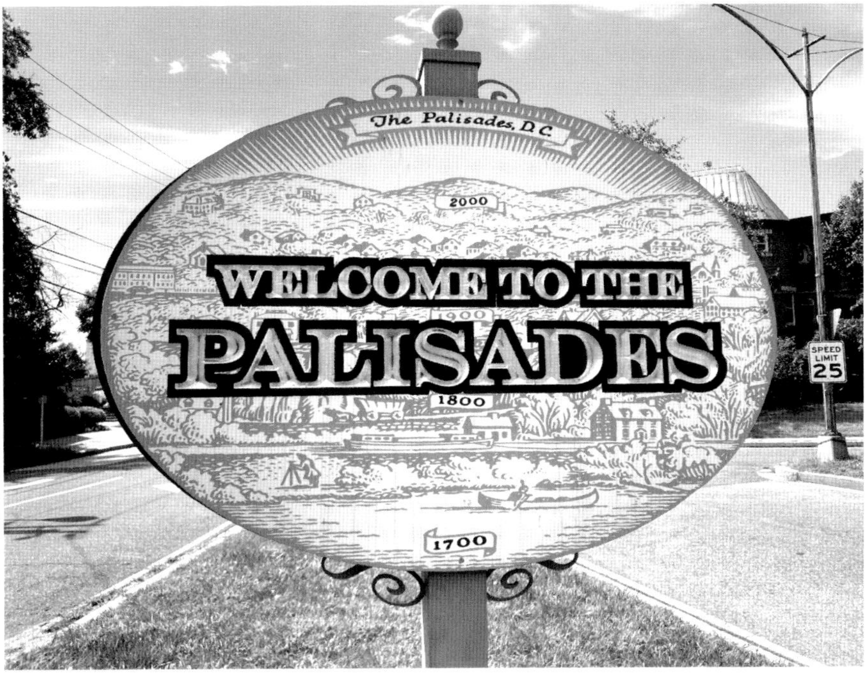

Above: Palisades Neighborhood Welcome Sign. *Photo by author.*

Right: Doug Dupin. *Courtesy of Doug Dupin.*

As Dupin has pointed out, archaeological investigations before construction work are required only if the site is owned by the city or the federal government. Most development in the Palisades is done on privately owned land, and artifacts it may contain are commonly lost or destroyed during construction.

Amateur archaeologists are strongly criticized by professionals because they typically collect artifacts without a thorough record of the site and context in which the artifacts were found. Dupin had some training in archaeology in college. In his digs, Dupin attempts to record as much context as possible when collecting but defends the limitations of his efforts by calling it "salvage archaeology."[136]

Without time or resources to do the work that would be done by professionals, saving artifacts from being lost or destroyed is better than nothing and often the best he and others interested in preserving the past can do. As was noted in chapter 6, the Foggy Bottom area was probably once rich in artifacts from its past Native American occupation, but careless development has erased that history, except for a few sites around the periphery of the neighborhood.

In May 2021, Dupin worked with Palisades residents Alex Knott and Patrick Shaughness to incorporate the Palisades History Museum, which now includes Dupin's finds regarding the Palisades' Native American history. It also covers the history of the development of the Palisades neighborhood through the Civil War, into the twentieth century to the present. The nonprofit museum is seeking donations to fund the building or renting of a permanent home for its collections. You can learn more at its website, the Palisades History Museum, https://www.palisadeshistory.org/.

As with other nearby areas, the assortment of stone points and pottery that have been found in the Palisades indicates that the area was occupied over thousands of years before European colonists arrived. The Native Americans who lived there used stone such as rhyolite, a stone not sourced locally, and they left ceramic remains from tribes that had come to the lower falls area of the Potomac from distant parts of the mid-Atlantic region and inland from the Atlantic coast. As noted earlier, the rich abundance of fish and other food sources of the lower Potomac had long been important resources for the survival of Native American people here and throughout the mid-Atlantic.

A RARE NATIVE HISTORY MARKER IN THE PALISADES

It is important to note that there is a rare marker that can be found in the Palisades. As part of the redevelopment and construction of a playground in Carolina Park, the DC Department of Parks and Recreation posted a marker sign regarding the archaeology and (Native) history in the Palisades. It can be found at the Macomb Street entrance to Carolina Park, overlooking the playground area.

It's odd that the sign doesn't include information on artifacts found at the Carolina Park site,[137] but it describes a wide range of items, including artifacts that were found at digs in the nearby Palisades Recreation Park. The marker even shows the Native bowl that was found on the grounds of JBAB (chapter 11). Despite the limitations of the Carolina Park sign, it is a rare public marker placed by a DC city agency acknowledging Native American history.

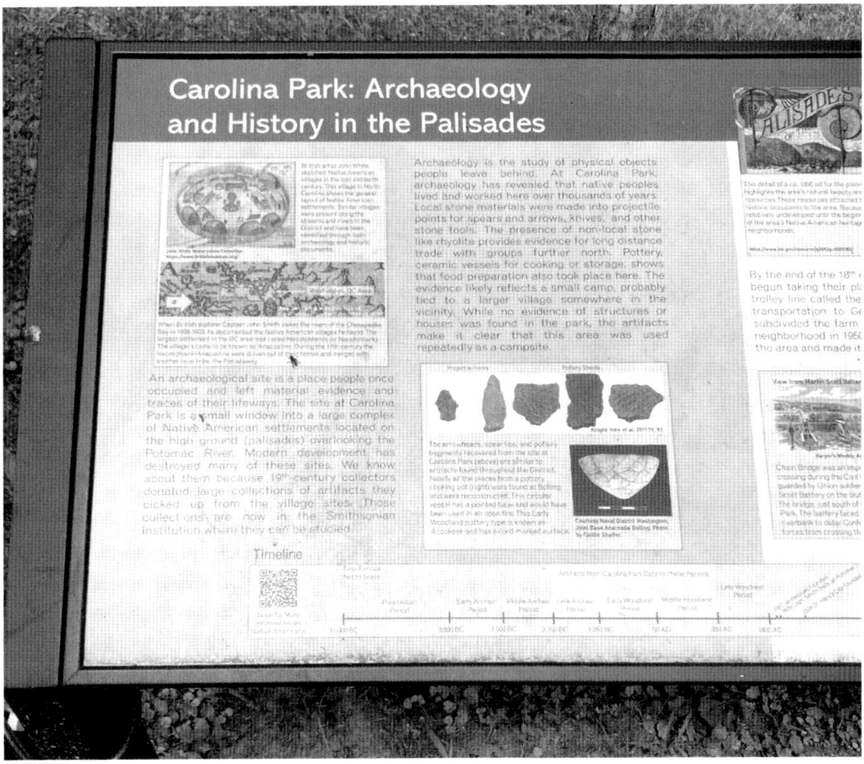

Native history sign, Carolina Park. *Photo by author.*

EPILOGUE

WHY IS NATIVE AMERICAN HISTORY OVERLOOKED IN DC? WHAT CAN WE DO?

As we've seen in the previous chapters, the major sites of Native American history in Washington, DC, are uncelebrated and unmarked. There is no monument or park named for the Anacostans. All too frequently, I've been told by DC residents, even those from Anacostia, that they didn't know that the Anacostan Natives were the source of the names for the river and southeast neighborhood.

The 1918 complaint by Margaret Downing, quoted at the opening of this book, about the indifference of Washingtonians to the original owners of the land on which the city was built, certainly remains true today.

Before considering some possible factors that explain this indifference and what concerned people might do to improve our situation, I want to cite a recent personal experience that showed me how persistent negative attitudes still are toward explaining our Native American history.

In the early summer of 2022, I was contacted by an intern for a major land conservancy in Washington. The land is still largely undeveloped, and the Native presence on that land is one of many in Washington that have been detailed online by the National Park Service. The intern asked if I would be willing to do a presentation to a group of interested residents she planned to organize. I, of course, agreed, and we planned a meeting to discuss details two days later.

When we met, the intern explained with embarrassment that on the previous day she had described her plan at a staff meeting and was told by her supervisor that it shouldn't be done. As she put it, her supervisor said, "No." She went on to say that it was odd that later in the meeting they discussed a plan to teach about the Civil War history of the parkland. During our meeting, I suggested some possible indirect approaches the intern might try—like telling the story of fish runs in nearby streams and how the Natives took advantage of those fish runs. After our meeting, however, when the intern got back to me, she couldn't report any success with her efforts. Her comment was, "Now they definitely know about it. Maybe next year."

In my experience, I seem to hear "next year" all too frequently. This incident showed me how factors even stronger than indifference still seem to influence the programming of public groups in DC.

In the following discussion, in order to present more than my own perspective, I've collected quotes and comments from other Washingtonians about why Native American history is so overlooked in DC.

A 2004 *Washington Post* article that mostly discussed uncovering remains from a stable that was once used at the White House also mentioned a few Native American sites around the city, including the burial site uncovered near the Whitehurst Freeway (chapter 6).[138] For background and perspective on the archaeology done about Native American life in Washington, the reporter interviewed and quoted Stephen Potter, who was then chief archaeologist for the National Park Service's National Capital Region: "Potter said he is often surprised by how little Washingtonians know about the history of their city, particularly when it comes to its prehistoric past. 'It's as though they still believe the history of Washington began with the L'Enfant Plan.'"

There were an additional four sources I contacted for comments on Washington's attitudes toward our Native history.

Bob Engelman, who wrote the 1986 *Washington Post* article on the Native history of DC,[139] noted that it's not uncommon for people not to know much about their past, and in a transient city like DC, with a relatively large international population and a constant churn of political leaders (and followers), it's not surprising that there's even less attention in the DC area to the deep past, including to the Indigenous peoples who inhabited this land before they encountered Europeans.

In a recorded interview with David Silverman,[140] the author of *This Land Is Their Land*, and a personal interview with David Grosso, the former DC councilman who was the first to use a Native land acknowledgement before his city council meetings, they both pointed to one common factor

David Grosso. *Courtesy of David Grosso.*

that may explain why our Native American history is overlooked: an underlying shame or embarrassment regarding what was done to the Natives in our colonial history. Acknowledgement of that history presents the fact that this was the land of the Native people, and it was taken from them.

In my very enjoyable interview with David Grosso, I found his comments so insightful that I'll quote them extensively. For example, Grosso also drew parallels with the way that the history of slavery in Washington—a history that included their work building the White House—was erased and long overlooked.

> *You're seeing this also happen in current times trying to erase slavery from our history trying to erase the pain caused by slavery.*

Grosso also commented on the irony that in a progressive city like Washington, Native Americans were used as a mascot for the football team:

> *DC is a progressive place where people believe in human rights and stood up for human rights and yet it took how many years to get the name of the football team changed.*

In the spring of 2022, a friend of the DC Native History Project and creator of the Hill is Home website (https://thehillishome.com/) Maria Helena Carey brought a proposal to the Ward 6 Area Neighborhood Commission (ANC) that the name of Garfield Park be amended to include the Anacostans, who have a well-documented history on that land (chapter 2). Charles Allen, the Ward 6 DC councilman, informed the ANC that if the proposal was approved, he would bring it before the full city council for a vote that would put it in effect.

Unfortunately, however, after several ANC meetings where the basis for the change was fully explained, a subcommittee for the ANC district that included the park voted against the name change to "Garfield-Anacostan Park." As I pointed out, residents would not have to change the way that they referred to the park. They could still just say "Garfield Park," and the name change would not cause confusion. But two residents voiced opposition to the new name, and the proposition was defeated. This would have been the only site in Washington, DC, that would have included the

Anacostan name, and lead to the name being included on public maps of the District. In the future, as an alternative to renaming, the DCNHP is planning an augmented reality app that will show the park with the alternate name and explain its history to interested visitors. This certainly isn't comparable to getting the name on public maps, but for now it may be the most that can be done.

John Capozzi, a former shadow DC representative, made a brief reply to my question about DC's interest in its Native history that focused on the absence of the Anacostans in the National Museum of the American Indian (NMAI):

> *The fact that the National Museum of the American Indian has refused the honor that legacy has compounded that slight.*

Frankly, I'm bewildered by the situation in DC! When the NMAI opened in 2004, a blessing ritual was performed by Chief Billy Tayac, Turkey Tayac's son, then leader of the Piscataway Indian Nation. The NMAI does have an exhibit on the Natives of the Chesapeake. It covers the Piscataways, among several other tribes, but the map of where the Piscataway lived stops at the east side of the Anacostia and leaves the bulk of land that is now DC unmarked. The Anacostans are mentioned only to explain the name of the Anacostia River.

As I mention as often as possible when speaking publicly, to make the topic as embarrassing as possible to the NMAI,

> *Why don't they tell the story of the Native Anacostans, who once walked the land where the museum now sits?*

In 2018, I came across a publication of the NMAI, which has a museum in New York City as well as Washington. The article that I found online was "Manahatta to Manhattan," an excellent retelling of the Native American people of the Lenape tribe who once lived in Manhattan.[141] In a letter I wrote to Kevin Grover on October 15, 2018, I cited that document on the Manahatta and pointed out that it contrasts sharply with the absence of a similar story about the Native tribe of Washington, DC.[142] Oddly, when I later went back to look for the Manahatta document, I found it was no longer available on the website of the NMAI. It can still be viewed online from a website in Washington State.[143] I don't know of an explanation for why the NMAI deleted it. I'm reluctant to take "credit" for making it happen.

In November 2018, when people at the NMAI were asked about the absence of Anacostan Native history by *Washington Post* reporter Dana Hedgpeth, who is Native American, Ann McMullen, a supervisory museum curator, said exhibits are designed to

> *focus on living people and not on Anacostans who have been absorbed into other tribes.*[144]

Of course, the various Piscataway tribes intermarried over the long period they lived here. But the history of the Piscataway/Anacostans in Washington is not being told at the NMAI or on its website. The comments from the NMAI in that *Washington Post* story suggesting that there were no Piscataways to represent the Anacostan tribe upset Chief Jesse James Swann of the Piscataway Conoy Tribe (http://www.piscatawaytribe.org/) so much, he contacted me. That began our work together on telling the story of the Piscataway/Anacostans in and around Washington, DC, which he mentioned in his foreword and is described in more detail below.

The NMAI must also explain why they aren't telling the stories of the numerous sites around the city that relate not only to the Anacostans but also to the thousands of Native American people who lived, quarried and were buried on land that is now Washington. As the previous chapters have detailed, the Native Americans who migrated into this area, with their dogs, have lived here for thousands of years and left a variety of artifacts that reflect their history, including the storage pits found at Fletcher's Cove and the arrowheads and pottery found on the White House grounds. There are many Native stories to be told in this city, including those left by the Anacostans.

As Bob Engelman commented, most people don't know much about their personal histories, let alone the history of the land they live on. In my case, I had lived in Washington for more than thirty years before I was prompted by my travels to Australia to begin searching the Indigenous history of Washington.

When I began my searches, one of the first resources I found that includes an excellent retelling of the history of the Anacostans is the 2017 book *Chocolate City*, by Chris Myers Asch and George Derek Musgrove.[145] Peter Ufland mentions this book in his foreword but didn't draw attention to how the authors gave a thorough treatment of the racial and cultural history of the city by rightfully starting with an account of the English settlers' interactions with the Anacostan tribe in the 1600s.

Responsibility for developing an awareness and teaching about our Native history falls on the cultural institutions in our city. As stated here repeatedly, the NMAI isn't telling those stories. As another prominent example, the DC History Center (https://dchistory.org/about/history/), is dedicated to collect and preserve the history of Washington *only* since it became a city. The *Washington History Magazine*, which has been in publication under various titles since 1894, has published only one article on the Native American History of DC, in 1923.[146]

As discussed in chapter 9, public acknowledgement of the extensive Native American history that has been documented on the Joint Base Anacostia-Bolling will be an important step in raising awareness of the Native history of the entire Washington, DC region. Understanding that the Anacostan chief and his tribe once lived so close to the center of the city and had a burial ground there will help bring to life the story of the Anacostans. If developed suitably, the land on and nearby the base could be a site that provides a rich connection with the Native history of our city for students, DC residents and our many visitors.

However, in contrast with the preceding groups that have not publicly acknowledged their Native history, the DC Public Library (DCPL) has begun offering a variety of important programs and materials to the people of the District. Each November for the last few years, the DCPL has featured a variety of books and online sources about local Native American history during Native American Heritage Month. In November 2020, they organized a land acknowledgement ceremony to mark the reopening of the main Martin Luther King building, which is available on the library's website. As you can see by viewing an online video of the event, the participants included Chief Swann of the Piscataway Conoy Tribe and Julie Tayac Yates, the matriarch of the Piscataway Indian Nation, the two tribes that were officially recognized by the State of Maryland in 2012.

Despite this one positive institutional development at the DCPL, the case is all too clear that not enough is being done to educate and celebrate the Native American history of Washington.

Let's move on to discuss how this might be changed.

What can be done?

Well, the situation is clear—the Native American history of Washington, DC, has been neglected and essentially erased from public view. The big question before us is, "What can be done?"

My conversation with David Grosso brought him to suggest several useful strategies to produce change. Here's his general advice:

> *It takes more and more engagement from everyday people who care about human rights to say this is not right. Advocate with what you purchase and where you visit and the things that you do.*

This is advice from the man who led the way by using a Native land acknowledgement to open his DC City council meetings. You can rest assured he recommends more people use these acknowledgements!

> *People can demand that we say where we are.... Wherever you're meeting, if it's public at all, you should recognize the land that you're standing on.*

Here's the Native Land Acknowledgement I put together with Chief Swann in 2019, which was used by David Grosso:

> *We acknowledge that this meeting is taking place on the traditional land of the Anacostan People of the Piscataway Tribe. We pay respect to their Chiefs and Elders both past and present.*

This is a basic land acknowledgement that can be used at any group meeting in Washington. It is a call to remind all present of our Native tribe. It's been encouraging to get reports from friends that Native land acknowledgements have been done at public events put on by the Smithsonian Institution and before plays performed by the Folger Shakespeare Theater.

It's an open question about the size and nature of the group in which you might choose to include a Native land acknowledgement. I've heard stories that some people in Australia include a land acknowledgement at their dinner parties. In the hope of offsetting the erasure of our Native American history, I'd say Native land acknowledgements can't be used too much!

In the fall of 2022, I was excited to be contacted by a DC resident who wanted help designing a plaque for her new sidewalk in NE, which would include a land acknowledgement. Her daughter had shown a great interest in Native American life when she was four years old, which had gotten her and her husband much more aware of Native history. When their sidewalk was replaced, they included a plaque that did just that. Let's hope that this story prompts others in DC to make a literal "concrete" effort regarding Native land acknowledgements.

Land acknowledgement sidewalk plaque. *Photo by author.*

A group that's not based in the Washington, DC area, the U.S. Department of Art and Culture, is an excellent resource for information on Native land acknowledgements. They have worked with a diverse group of Native Americans to assemble an extensive document on Native land acknowledgements that is available online.[147] Also, this excellent Canadian website, Native Land Digital (https://native-land.ca/), will help readers identify the Indigenous people of their location, not only for the continental United States but also locations around the world.

I've heard comments by Native Americans who are frustrated by the use of Native land acknowledgements because they don't seem to be productive of real change. I'll leave commentary on these frustrations to Native Americans, but I want voice my perspective on the importance of gestures like land acknowledgements that have brought some real changes to the lives of Native Americans.

Simply stated, the people of America have been silent, and sadly kept ignorant, of many fundamental facts on Native American history. The wealthy, often corporate groups, that do own and control the land in this country don't want to hear about this embarrassing fact—much like the naked emperor in Hans Christian Anderson's folktale didn't want to know he was being a fool. We live in a capitalist world where the people of the country are courted for their buying power. If enough people take interest in an issue—in this case, the Native American history of our land—that becomes something that needs a corporate response.

In the spring of 2022, I was contacted by Kerrien Suarez, president of the group Equity in the Center (https://equityinthecenter.org/). They work with organizations, many in the philanthropic community, to help raise awareness of internal equity issues and promote the use of organizational structures that are free of bias regarding race, ethnicity and gender. Kerrien's group wanted to identify a local Native tribe so they could begin to make annual donations as a "rent/a tax…to support land back initiatives and/or any immediate (community) needs."[148]

Here is an excellent, creative way to respond to our collective awareness of the Native history of our land. It's a response that is being made in the context of our growing awareness of our Native history, and it likely would not have happened if the topic hadn't been repeatedly invoked in land acknowledgements. Details of how this group decided to give their support to local Native Americans are explained below.

What else can be done? It's also important to stay aware of the work being done by our local Native tribe, the Piscataway Conoy Tribe. You can visit their website (http://www.piscatawaytribe.org/) and their Facebook page to find details on their latest activities.

David Grosso also mentioned the importance of financially supporting our local Native people: "People who have the means can donate…and make sure that these folks that are left behind are remembered."

Chief Swann has organized a 501(c)3 organization, "Through Piscataway Eyes" (TPE) (https://www.throughpiscatawayeyes.org), to accept donations "to promote and protect the welfare, culture, and history of the members of the Piscataway Conoy Tribe."

Part of TPE is the Piscataway Land Trust,™ which is structured "to accept land donations and/or monetary donations to purchase land to benefit all future generations of Piscataway people."

You can find details about how to make donations on the TPE website.

In the interest of paying rent to local Native Americans and supporting land buy-back initiatives, Equity in the Center announced on its blog in the fall of 2022 that they would be donating 2 percent of their annual budget to TPE. Let's hope that their excellent annual contributions prompt other groups to follow their example.

One last focus that was noted by David Grosso was, "Demand it [local Native history] be taught in schools!"

I was recently involved in an effort to get details on local Native American history to teachers in the public schools of DC. In August 2022, I was invited to do a presentation on "The Hidden Native History of Washington, DC" to DC public school teachers during their orientation for the fall 2022 school year.

Previously, this wasn't a topic that got included in the teaching plans for DC public schools.

Native fishing license presentation by Tommy Wells, director of the Department of Energy and Environment, to Matriarch Julie Tayac Yates and Chief Jesse James Swann, October 15, 2022. *Photo by author.*

There are also many charter and private schools in Washington, DC. If you have children in one of them, or teach there, ask what is being taught about the local Native American history. Please tell the school administrators about how you came to ask them these questions and direct them to this book or the DC Native History Project, if they would like more information.

Closing Statement

No Place to Go but Up!

If you've read this book, you've learned about the major sites of DC's Native American history and some of the options available to concerned Washingtonians. Now, we must all begin doing our part to get out word about the Native History of this city!

During the last decade, while I've collected the Native American history of Washington and attempted to spread awareness of that history, from time to time, when it seemed like no progress was being made, I've taken some weak consolation in the fact that "there is no place to go but up!" There have been signs of progress. David Grosso introduced Native acknowledgements to the DC City Council. With backing from Councilman Charles Allen and David Grosso, the city council passed a bill to give free fishing rights to Piscataway tribe members, and those licenses became available on October 15, 2022. Large organizations, including DC Water and JBAB, have initiated plans to inform the public about the Native history of the lands they occupy. Native land acknowledgements are being used at some public events, and that list is growing. One DC family put a Native land acknowledgement on their new sidewalk. The Native history of DC is now being taught in some schools, and the DC Public Library has become a rich resource for teaching materials. Although the NMAI in Washington didn't include the history of the Anacostans or other Native sites in the first two decades of its existence, I believe those stories will eventually be told, either in the museum or online. I intend to keep bothering the NMAI until it happens. If you visit the museum, be sure to ask for information on the Anacostans and local Native sites—that will help prod them to tell those stories.

A major goal of this book has been to "arm" the reader with the stories and Native American history of Washington so you will be ready to do your part to get these stories told to the general public. And remember, if you get discouraged trying to get word out about DC's Native American history, keep in mind, "There is no place to go but up!"

Notes

Preface

1. Margaret Brent Downing, "The Earliest Proprietors of Capitol Hill," *Records of the Columbia Historical Society* 21 (1918): 1–23.
2. "Did Slaves Build the White House?" White House Historical Association, https://www.whitehousehistory.org/did-slaves-build-the-white-house.
3. REPROTOX® is a service of the Reproductive Toxicology Center, a nonprofit foundation, https://reprotox.org/about.
4. National Apology 2008, National Museum of Australia, https://www.nma.gov.au/defining-moments/resources/national-apology.
5. "Australia Marks 20-Year Anniversary of Sorry Day," SBS News, 2018. https://www.sbs.com.au/language/english/australia-marks-20-year-anniversary-of-sorry-day_1.
6. Tim O'Neil, "A Look Back • Big Mound in St. Louis, Legacy of a Lost Culture, Leveled in 1869," *St. Louis Post-Dispatch*, November 8, 2021, https://www.stltoday.com/news/archives/a-look-back-big-mound-in-st-louis-legacy-of-a-lost-culture-leveled-in/article_3b006339-444d-575f-91c5-8b4f96fa08cd.html.
7. Development of the United States Capital, Washington, GPA 1930 (Seventy-First Congress, First session, House Documebt no. 35), Library of the University of Michigan, F 199. D48. P. 6.
8. S.V. Proudfit, "Ancient Village Sites and Aboriginal Workshops in the District of Columbia, " 241–6. in Otis T. Mason, W.J. McGee, Thomas Wilson, S.V. Proudfit, W. H. Holmes, Elmer R. Reynolds and James Mooney, "The Aborigines of the District of Columbia and the Lower Potomac—A Symposium, Under the Direction of the Vice President of Section D," 241–6, *American Anthropologist* 2, no. 3 (1889): 225–68, http://www.jstor.org/stable/658373 [hereafter Mason et al., "Aborigines of the District"].

9. Once As It Was Map of Washington, DC, http://onceasitwasdc.org/index.html.
10. Don Hawkins, *Topography of the Federal City, 1791: [Washington D.C.]*, 1990, https://lccn.loc.gov/91684423.

1. How Did the Anacostans Get Their Name? Mistakes Were Made

11. Edward Wright Haile, ed., *Jamestown Narratives: Eyewitness Accounts of the Virginia Colony, The First Decade, 1607–1617* (Champlain, VA: RoundHouse, 2001).
12 "Captain John Smith," National Park Service, September 4, 2022, https://www.nps.gov/jame/learn/historyculture/life-of-john-smith.htm
13. "Queen Elizabeth I: Colonizing America," Royal Museums Greenwich, https://www.rmg.co.uk/stories/topics/queen-elizabeth-i-colonising-america.
14. "Captain John Smith."
15. Haile, *Jamestown Narratives*, 84.
16. Ibid., 198.
17. J.A. Leo Lemay, *Did Pocahontas Save Captain John Smith?* (Athens: University of Georgia Press, 1992).
18. Philip L. Barbour, ed., *The Complete Works of Captain John Smith*, 3 vols. (Chapel Hill: University of North Carolina Press, 2011), 1:227.
19. "John Smith's Map of Virginia: A Closer Look," National Park Service, https://www.nps.gov/articles/000/smith-map-of-virginia.htm.
20. William Wallace Tooker, "On the Meaning of the Name Anacostia," *American Anthropologist* 7, no. 4 (October 1894): 389–93.
21. "Nacotchtank," Wikipedia, May 2023, https://en.wikipedia.org/wiki/Nacotchtank. Note: The wiki spelling is not the same as seen on the map. Anacostine is a variation of Anacostan, with an added *i*, which does not occur in any of the original forms of the name.
22. Tooker, "On the Meaning of the Name," 390–1.
23. James Mooney, "Indian Tribes of the District of Columbia," in Mason et al., "Aborigines of the District," 259–68.
24. Louise D. Hutchinson, *The Anacostia Story, 1608–1930* (Washington: Published for the Anacostia Neighborhood Museum of the Smithsonian Institution by the Smithsonian Institution Press, 1977), 27, https://library.si.edu/digital-library/book/anacostiastor1600hutc.
25. J. Edwards, *Observations of the Language of the Muhhekaneew Indians. Communicated to the Connecticut Society of Arts and Sciences* (New Haven, CT: Josiah Meigs, 1787).
26. Archives of Maryland Online, *Proceedings and Acts of the General Assembly* vol. 2, p. 25, https://msa.maryland.gov/megafile/msa/speccol/sc2900/sc2908/000001/000002/html/am2--25.html
27. G. Tayac, "Keeping the Original Instructions," in *Native Universe: Voices of Indian America*, ed. Gerald McMaster (Washington, DC: National Museum of the American Indian, 2004), 77–78; Haile, *Jamestown Narratives*, 2001.

2. The Native Village Five Blocks from the U.S. Capitol

28. Scott Longert, "Friends to the End," National Park Service, https://www.nps.gov/articles/000/friends-to-the-end.htm.
29. "Indian Remains, Etc., Found. What the Workmen Grading a Public Reservation Have Dug Up," *Evening Star*, August 22, 1883.
30. "Some Curious Discoveries. An Indian Girl's Skeleton and Other Relics of the Past," *Washington Post*, August 12, 1883.
31. "Indian Remains, Etc., Found."
32. "Some Curious Discoveries."
33. O'Neil, "Look Back."
34. Lori Wysong, "L'Enfante's Guide to Getting Fired," Boundary Stones, August 2, 2019, https://boundarystones.weta.org/2019/08/02/lenfants-guide-getting-fired.
35. Proudfit, "Ancient Village Sites," 241.
36. S.V. Proudfit, "A Collection of Stone Implements from the District of Columbia," *Proceedings of United States National Museum* 18, no 810 (1890): 189.
37. Rebecca Seib and Helen C. Rountree, *Indians of Southern Maryland* (Baltimore: Maryland Historical Society, 2014), 19; "Indian Towns," Virtual Jamestown, https://virtual-jamestown.com/home/indian-towns/.
38. Proudfit, "Collection of Stone Implements," 189.
39. S.V. Proudfit, "Aboriginal Occupancy of the District of Columbia," *Records of the Columbia Historical Society* 25 (1923): 191.
40. Proudfit journal online, compare http://n2t.net/ark:/65665/32db7aadb-4a2b-47e7-a343-c680259e034f and http://n2t.net/ark:/65665/3045f4c3a-c921-49a7-bb42-bac81a893b8c.

3. The Anacostans and Their Dogs

41. "Captain John Smith."
42. "The Lost Colony of Roanoke: The Tale of Virginia Dare," Outer Banks of North Carolina, https://www.outerbanks.org/things-to-do/museums-and-historic-sites/the-lost-colony-outdoor-drama/.
43. Jeffrey P. Blick, "The Archaeology and Ethnohistory of the Dog in Virginia Algonquian Culture as Seen from Weyanoke Old Town," in *Papers of the Thirty-First Algonquian Conference*, ed. John D. Nichols, 1–17 (Winnipeg: University of Manitoba Press, 2000).
44. Ibid., 3.
45. Helen C Rountree, "Uses of Domesticated Animals by Early Virginia Indians," Encyclopedia Virginia, https://www.encyclopediavirginia.org/Domesticated_Animals_During_the_Pre-Colonial_Era.
46. Phyllis Beasley, "Trainers Visit S.C.'s Original Native Dog," *Columbia Star*, August 11, 2017, https://www.thecolumbiastar.com/articles/trainers-visit-s-c-s-original-native-dog/.

47. "Carolina Dog," American Rare Breed Association, https://web.archive.org/web/20150603172156/http://www.arba.org/carolina-dog.htm.
48. J. Hitt, "DNA Backs Lore on Pre-Columbian Dogs," *New York Times*, July 16, 2013, https://www.nytimes.com/2013/07/16/science/a-dog-that-goes-way-back.html.
49. M. Ní Leathlobhair, A.R. Perri, E.K. Irving-Pease, et al., "The Evolutionary History of Dogs in the Americas," *Science* 361, no. 6397 (2018): 81–85, doi: 10.1126/science.aao4776.
50. Ruth Callahan, "Domestication of Dogs and Their Use on the Great Plains," *Nebraska Anthropologist* 14 (1997): 103, https://digitalcommons.unl.edu/nebanthro/103.

4. The Native American Quarries in Northwest Washington, DC

51. William H. Holmes, "A Quarry Workshop of the Flakes-Stone Implement Makers in the District of Columbia," *American Anthropologist* 3, no. 1 (January 1890): 3.
52. Titus Ulke, "Indian Workshops Once Located Here: Washington Was Once One of the…" *Washington Post*, September 23, 1934.
53. Holmes, "Quarry Workshop of the Flakes," 2.
54. William H. Holmes, "Excavations in an Ancient Soapstone Quarry in the District of Columbia," *American Anthropologist* 3, no. 4 (October 1890): 321–30.
55. Ann Kessler, "Lost Forest Hills: The Rose Hill Quarry," Forest Hills Connection, December 12, 2019, https://www.foresthillsconnection.com/news/lost-forest-hills-the-rose-hill-quarry/
56. Elmer R. Reynolds, *Aboriginal Soapstone Quarries in the District of Columbia* (Forgotten Books, 2018), 527.
57. Peabody Museum Research for Soapstone artifacts: Enter https://collections.peabody.harvard.edu/collections. In the "Search the collection" window, enter "78-59*".

5. The Native American Artifacts Found on the White House Grounds in the 1970s

58. Caitlin Daday, "Presidential History of Swimming," *Swimming World*, February 21, 2022, https://www.swimmingworldmagazine.com/news/the-presidential-history-of-swimming/.
59. Robert Humphrey and Mary Elizabeth Chambers, *Ancient Washington: American Indian Cultures of the Potomac Valley.* (Washington, DC: George Washington University, 1977).
60. "Captain John Smith."
61. Humphrey and Chambers, *Ancient Washington*, 30–31.
62. Robert Engelman, "Washington Before Washington," *Washington Post Magazine*, July 1986.

63. Dana Hedgpeth, "A Native American Tribe Once Called D.C. Home. It's Had No Living Members for Centuries," *Washington Post*, November 22, 2018, https://www.washingtonpost.com/history/2018/11/22/native-american-tribe-once-called-dc-home-its-had-no-living-members-centuries/.
64. Lina Mann, "Before the White House," White House Historical Association, https://www.whitehousehistory.org/before-the-white-house.
65. Tatyana Hopkins, "GW Develops a 'Guide to Indigenous D.C.,'" GWToday, July 8, 2019, https://gwtoday.gwu.edu/gw-develops-%E2%80%98guide-indigenous-dc%E2%80%99.
66. Humphrey and Chambers, *Ancient Washington*, 31.

6. Foggy Bottom Burial Site and Artifacts Found in 1997

67. Whitehurst Freeway Historical Overview, "Eastern Roads," http://www.dcroads.net/roads/whitehurst/.
68. National Historic Preservation Act of 1966, "National Conference of State Historic Preservation Officers (NCSHPO)," https://ncshpo.org/resources/national-historic-preservation-act-of-1966/.
69. Dennis Knepper, John M. Rutherford, Daniel R. Hayes, et al., *The Archaeology of an Urban Landscape, The Whitehurst Freeway Archaeological Project*, vol. 1, *Prehistoric Sites* (Washington, DC: District of Columbia Department of Transportation, 2006). https://www.studypool.com/documents/13859590/the-archaeology-of-an-urban-landscape-the-whitehurst-freeway-archaeological-project-pdfdrive-.
70. "Prehistoric Landscapes of the Nation's Capital: Rock Creek Park," National Park Service, https://www.nps.gov/articles/prehistoric-landscapes-of-the-nation-s-capital.htm.
71. Alia Dastagir, "Behind the Name: Foggy Bottom," dcist, November 6, 2011, https://dcist.com/story/11/11/06/behind-the-name-foggy-bottom/.

7. Henry Fleete: The Young Man Who Lived with the Anacostans for Five Years in the 1620s

72. "First Hand Accounts," Virtual Jamestown, http://www.virtualjamestown.org/exist/cocoon/jamestown/fha/J1040.
73. Henry Spelman, *Relation of Virginia* (London: Jas. F. Hunnewell at the Chiswick Press, 1872), https://content.wisconsinhistory.org/digital/collection/aj/id/8665/.
74. Stephen R. Potter, *Commoners, Tribute, and Chiefs: the Development of Algonquian Culture in the Potomac Valley* (Charlottesville: University Press of Virginia, 1993).
75. Henry Fleete journal, 1631–1632, 19–20, the Peter Force Collection Series 7E, item 27, Library of Congress, https://lccn.loc.gov/mm82067884.
76. Betsy Fleet, *Henry Fleete: Pioneer, Explorer, Trader, Planter, Legislator, Justice & Peacemaker* (Richmond, VA: B. Fleet, 1989).
77. Potter, *Commoners, Tribue, and Chiefs*, 187.
78. Fleet, *Henry Fleete*.

79. Ibid., 20–11.
80. Charles C. Mann, *1491: New Revelations of the Americas before Columbus* (New York: Knopf, 2005).
81. Fleet, *Henry Fleete.*

8. The U.S. National Arboretum Native Village Site

82. Proudfit journal online
83. Proudfit, "Ancient Village Sites," 243.
84. Robert Malesky, "A Home for America's Bad Boys," Bygone Brookland, October 9, 2017, https://bygonebrookland.com/2017/10/09/a-home-for-americas-bad-boys/.
85. Register of Historic Places Nomination Form, National Arboretum, https://npgallery.nps.gov/GetAsset/8a212300-4883-4dfc-a7c6-81acd4377aca.
86. "Colored CCC Camp Here Wins Honor Rating for This Area," *Washington Evening Star*, April 4, 1940.
87. Register of Historic Places Nomination Form, National Arboretum.

9. The Anacostan Chief's Village and Native Burial Grounds—Now the Anacostia-Bolling Military Base

88. Seib and Rountree, *Indians of Southern Maryland.*
89. Barbour, *Complete Works of Captain John Smith*, 2:105.
90. Ibid., 1:167.
91. Ibid., 1:228.
92. William Hand Browne, *George Calvert and Cecilius Calvert: Barons Baltimore of Baltimore* (New York: Dodd, Mead and Company), 35–36.
93. Paul Byron Cissna, "The Piscataway Indians of Southen Maryland: An Ethnohistory from Pre-European Contact to the Present (Late Woodland, Chesapeake Bay, Algonquian" (PhD diss., American University, 1986), https://www.proquest.com/openview/c70b3dc3bbdd7980795030f31354ddc7/1?cbl=18750&diss=y&pq-origsite=gscholar.
94. A. Herrman, H. Faithorne and T. Withinbrook, *Virginia and Maryland as It Is Planted and Inhabited This Present Year* (London: 1673), map retrieved from the Library of Congress, https://www.loc.gov/item/2002623131/.
95. "The Growth of the Tobacco Trade," U.S. History, https://www.ushistory.org/us/2d.asp.
96. "Giesboro Point Cavalry Depot, Parking for 30,000 Horses," Civil War Washington, D.C., August 17, 2011, http://civilwarwashingtondc1861-1865.blogspot.com/2011/08/geisborough-point-cavalry-depot-parking.html.
97. Proudfit, "Ancient Village Sites," 242.
98. "History of Joint Base Anacostia-Bolling," Joint Base Anacostia-Bolling, https://www.jbab.jb.mil/About-JBAB/.

99. T.D. Stewart and W.R. Wedel, "The Finding of Two Ossuaries on the Site of the Indian Village of Nacotchtanke (Anacostia)," *Journal of the Washington Academy of Sciences* 27, no. 5 (1937): 213–19.
100. "Ancient Cemetery in Anacostia Yields Bones Held Prehistoric," *Washington Post*, September 11, 1936.
101. "Skeletons Unearthed at Bolling Field," *Washington Evening Star*, September 11, 1936.
102. Stewart and Wedel, "Finding of Two Ossuaries."
103. "History of Joint Base Anacostia-Bolling."
104. Karis Lee, "Skeletons in the Closet: The Smithsonian's Native American Remains and the NMAI," Boundary Stones, https://boundarystones.weta.org/2020/05/21/skeletons-closet-smithsonian%E2%80%99s-native-american-remains-and-founding-national-museum.

10. The Native Canoe Found near the Navy Yard and the Native Fishing Site Found next to Washington, DC's New Soccer Stadium

105. "Condensed Locals," *Washington Evening Star*, August 15, 1871.
106. B. Arnebeck, *Through a Fiery Trial. Building Washington 1790–1800* (Lanham, MD: Madison Books, 1991).
107. "Memento of the Past," *National Republican*, August 14, 1871.
108. "The James Creek Canal," *Washington Evening Star*, December 20, 1866.

11. Anacostia Metro and Barney Circle Artifacts, the Native Pot Found in 2009

109. P. James, "The History of Settlement and Land Use along the Eastern Branch," in *East of the River: Continuity and Change*, ed. Gail Lowe, 18–49 (Washington, DC: Smithsonian, Anacostia Community Museum, 2010).
110. "Prehistoric Rocks and Stones Shaped by Human Hands," Anacostia Community Museum, https://anacostia.si.edu/collection/object/acm_1991.0064.0003a.
111. National Conference of State Historic Preservation Officers (NCSHPO), 1966.
112. V. Loeb, "Norton Declares Barney Circle Freeway a Dead End," *Washington Post*, March 5, 1997.
113. *Prehistoric Life Along the Anacostia River: Archaeology at the Barney Circle Sites* (DC SHPO Archaeological Report #560 Booklet: Versar, 2013), 11.
114. Ibid., 24.
115. NCSHPO, 1966.
116. G. Katz, "Bellevue's Telltale Heart (51SW7): Accokeek Under the Floorboards," paper presented at Middle Atlantic Archaeological Conference, Ocean City, MD, https://www.academia.edu/10648132/Bellevue_s_Telltale_Heart_51SW7_Accokeek_Under_The_Floorboards

117. "Prehistoric Ceramics," Maryland Archaeological Conservation Lab, https://apps.jefpat.maryland.gov/diagnostic/PrehistoricCeramics/earlywoodlandperiod.html.
118. Caitlin E.R. Shaffer, "An Accokeek Pot," Maryland Archaeological Conservation Laboratory, https://jefpat.maryland.gov/Pages/mac-lab/curators-choice/2011-curators-choice/2011-07-an-accokeek-pot.aspx.
119. Katz, "Bellevue's Telltale Heart."
120. D. DeSimone, "A History of Military Service: Native Americans in the U.S. Military Yesterday and Today," USO, https://www.uso.org/stories/2914-a-history-of-military-service-native-americans-in-the-u-s-military-yesterday-and-today.

12. Sites Near the Potomac River: Native Storage Pits at Fletcher's Cove, the Maddox Branch Sites and the Palisades Neighborhood

121. Tayac, "Keeping the Original Instructions," 77.
122. NCSHPO, 1966.
123. L. Wheeler, "Mysterious Silos Found Next to C&O Canal: Underground Pits Are 2,000 Years Old," *Washington Post*, November 1, 1998.
124. W.P. Barse, *An Archeological Survey, Inventory and Evaluation Study, and Data Recovery for the Fletcher's Boathouse Site (51NW13), C&O Canal National Historical Park, Washington, DC*, report submitted to National Park Service, National Capital Region, by URS Corporation.
125. Personal communication.
126. Barse, *Archeological Survey*, 53.
127. C.W. McNett, "The Potomac Avenue Site in Washington, D.C.," *Maryland Archeology* 8, no. 2 (1972): 23–35.
128. S. Fiedel, et al., 2008. "*Bold, Rocky, and Picturesque": Archeological Overview and Assessment and Archeological Identification and Evaluation Study of Rock Creek Park, District of Columbia*, vol. 2 (Washington, DC: Louis Berger Group, 2008).
129. Ibid., 9.
130. Ibid., 12.
131. R.E. Sterns, *The Hughes Site: An Aboriginal Village Site on the Potomac River in Montgomery County, Maryland*, Proceedings No. 6, https://apps.jefpat.maryland.gov/NEH/Assets/Collections/images/18mo01/PDFs/report_1940.pdf
132. C.A. Jirikowic, *Final Report on the 1990, 1991, and 1994 Excavations at the Hughes Site* (18MO1), American University, https://apps.jefpat.maryland.gov/NEH/Assets/Collections/images/18mo01/PDFs/final_report.pdf.
133. Proudfit, "Ancient Village Sites," 243.
134. McNett, "Potomac Avenue Site."
135. H. Hsu, "Just the Artifacts, Ma'am," *Washington City Paper*, October 13, 2006, https://washingtoncitypaper.com/article/238549/just-the-artifacts-maam/.
136. Ibid.
137. Doug Dupin, personal communication.

Epilogue: Why Is Native American History Overlooked in DC? What Can We Do?

138. A.L. Becker, "Below Ground, Washington's Lost History," *Washington Post*, July 8, 2004, https://www.washingtonpost.com/archive/local/2004/07/08/below-ground-washingtons-lost-history/57d35373-7ff6-43cf-bb48-2948512da6c9/.
139. Engelman, "Washington Before Washington," 1986.
140. Extended Interview with David J. Silverman, https://youtu.be/lvIoBqMhl70.
141. *Manahatta to Manhattan* (Office of the Superintendent of Public Instruction, Washington State, 2020), https://www.k12.wa.us/sites/default/files/public/indianed/tribalsovereignty/elementary/uselementary/uselementary-unit1/level2-materials/manahatta_to_manhattan.pdf.
142. Armand Lione, "The Absence of the Anacostan Natives of DC from the National Museum of the American Indian," https://nativevillagemarker.blogspot.com/2018/10/the-absence-of-anacostan-natives-of-dc.html
143. OSPI, 2022.
144. Hedgpeth, "Native American Tribe Once Called D.C. Home," 2018.
145. C.M. Asch, G.D. Musgrove, *Chocolate City: A History of Race and Democracy in the Nation's Capital* (Chapel Hill: University of North Caroline Press, 2017).
146. Proudfit, "Aboriginal Occupancy," 182–93.
147. "Honor Native Land: A Guide and Call to Acknowledgment," U.S. Department of Arts & Culture, https://usdac.us/nativeland.
148. Personal communication.

Index

T

U

W

Y

About the Author

Photo by Sara Willi.

Dr. Armand Lione began studying the history of the Native people of Washington, DC, after spending time in Australia, where the local Indigenous people are celebrated. Trained as a toxicologist, Dr. Lione has lived and worked in the city for over forty years, evaluating studies on the possible reproductive effects of thousands of agents. His research on Native history led him to uncover the many sites in Washington where evidence of previous Native occupation has been found. His work has connected him with local Piscataway leaders. Brief reports of his findings have previously been published in blogs, websites and news stories.